Especially for
Jean

From
Jeanne-Marie & Kent

Date
December, 2017

The *12 Days* of *Christmas* COOKBOOK

— 2017 Edition —

BARBOUR BOOKS
An Imprint of Barbour Publishing, Inc.

Written and compiled by Rebecca Currington in association with Snapdragon Group℠ Tulsa, OK.

ISBN 978-1-68322-218-7

Published by Barbour Books, an imprint of Barbour Publishing, Inc., P.O. Box 719, Uhrichsville, Ohio 44683, www.barbourbooks.com.

Our mission is to publish and distribute inspirational products offering exceptional value and biblical encouragement to the masses.

Member of the
Evangelical Christian
Publishers Association

Contents

Introduction

On the first day of Christmas my true love sent to me...

Take a deep breath and you can smell it in the air—those intoxicating, delicious, and unique fragrances of Christmas. The scent of fresh pine needles and candles, along with favorite dishes wafting from the kitchen, carry us back to childhood and all its delights. Those special family recipes are such a great part of the spirit of Christmas. This year we have included many recipes that have been handed down for generations. We hope they will bless you and your family as well.

Father God, help us always remember that the joy in Christmas is the joy of knowing that we have been reconciled with You through the birth and death of Your Son, Jesus—the greatest gift ever given. Amen.

On the first day of Christmas my true love sent to me. . .

An Appetizer on a Platter

Gifts of time and love
are surely the basic ingredients
of a truly merry Christmas.

Peg Bracken

Dear Father, as we gather with our friends and loved ones during the holiday season, we pray that our hearts would be bound together in thanks for the constant goodness and faithfulness You have poured out on us throughout the past year, as well as Your abundant blessings and care to come in the years ahead. Amen.

And the angel said unto them, Fear not: for, behold, I bring you good tidings of great joy, which shall be to all people.

LUKE 2:10

Dasher's Quick Dip

1 (8 ounce) package cream cheese

1 (16 ounce) bottle creamy Caesar dressing

6 mini carrots

6 celery sticks

1 small cucumber, sliced

In small bowl, mix together cream cheese and Caesar dressing until smooth and creamy. Serve with carrots, celery, and cucumbers.

YIELD: ABOUT 12 SERVINGS

Green Chili Roll Ups

1 (8 ounce) package cream cheese

1 cup sour cream

1 (4 ounce) can diced green chilies

8 (10 inch) flour tortillas

1 cup salsa

In small bowl, combine cream cheese, sour cream, and chilies. Blend well. Spread moderately over tortillas and roll up. Refrigerate until chilled. Slice into 1-inch rounds. Serve with salsa.

YIELD: 20 SERVINGS

Fiesta Holiday Dip

✳ · ✳ · · ✳ · ✳ · · ✳

2 (11 ounce) cans Mexi-corn

1 cup mayonnaise

8 ounces sour cream

10 ounces grated cheddar cheese

1 (4 ounce) can chopped green chilies

3 green onions, chopped

2 jalapeno peppers, chopped

1 (16 ounce) bag corn chips

Drain corn. Pour into large bowl. Add mayonnaise, sour cream, cheddar cheese, chilies, onion, and peppers. Blend well. Refrigerate until ready to serve with chips.

Yield: 8 servings

Sleigh Bites

* · * · * · * · *

20 cherry tomatoes

1 pound bacon, cooked and crumbled

½ cup mayonnaise

¼ cup chopped onion

3 tablespoons grated parmesan cheese

2 tablespoons chopped parsley

Cut tomatoes in half and hollow out seeds. Turn upside down to drain. Prepare filling by combining bacon, mayonnaise, onion, cheese, and parsley in a bowl. Fill each tomato half with filling and refrigerate until ready to serve.

YIELD: 40 BITES

Pimento Cheese Dip

* · * · * · * · *

2 cups shredded cheddar cheese

1 cup mayonnaise

2 teaspoons Worcestershire sauce

1 teaspoon mustard

3 tablespoons chopped pimento

1 teaspoon sugar

1 (12 ounce) bag chips

Place cheese, mayonnaise, Worcestershire sauce, mustard, pimento, and sugar in blender. Cover and process on chop setting until smooth and creamy. Refrigerate until ready to serve with chips.

YIELD: 2 CUPS

Pickled Cranberries

1 cup sugar

1 cup water

½ cup red wine vinegar

1 tablespoon pickling spice

4 cups fresh cranberries

In non-aluminum saucepan, combine sugar, water, vinegar, and pickling spice. Boil for 5 minutes. Add cranberries to syrup mixture and return to boil. Boil for 2 minutes. Cool. Chill cranberries in syrup.

YIELD: 1 QUART CRANBERRIES

Party Nibbles

❋ · ❋ · ❋ · ❋ · ❋

2 cups round oat cereal

2 cups wheat squares

2 cups pretzel sticks

1 cup shoestring potatoes

1 pound salted mixed nuts

1 teaspoon garlic salt

½ teaspoon onion salt

1 teaspoon seasoned salt

3 tablespoons Worcestershire sauce

2 cups butter, melted

In large bowl, toss together oat cereal, wheat squares, pretzel sticks, shoestring potatoes, and nuts. Stir seasonings into melted butter and pour over dry mixture, stirring well to coat. Spread out on parchment-lined cookie sheets. Bake at 250 degrees for 2 hours, stirring every half hour.

YIELD: 8 QUARTS

Smoked Oyster Dip

❋ · ❋ · ❋ · ❋ · ❋

1 (8 ounce) package cream cheese, softened

1½ cups mayonnaise

1 tablespoon lemon juice

⅛ teaspoon hot sauce

1 (4½ ounce) can chopped ripe black olives, drained

1 (3.6 ounce) can smoked oysters, drained and chopped

Using an electric mixer, beat cream cheese at medium speed. Add mayonnaise, lemon juice, and hot sauce. Beat until smooth. Add olives and oysters, stirring gently to combine. Serve with crackers.

YIELD: 3 CUPS

Holiday Salsa

1 (28 ounce) can diced tomatoes

1 (2 ounce) can chopped black
  olives

1 (2 ounce) can diced green chilies

3 green onions, chopped

3 tablespoons olive oil

1½ tablespoons red wine vinegar

½ teaspoon garlic salt

2 teaspoons hot sauce

½ teaspoon ground black pepper

Warm tortilla chips

In large bowl, combine tomatoes, olives, chilies, onions, oil, vinegar, garlic salt, hot sauce, and pepper. Blend well. Cover and refrigerate until ready to serve (at least 2 hours). Just before serving, pour chips onto cookie sheet and place in a 200-degree oven just until warm.

YIELD: 3 CUPS

Grandpa's Spectacular Sausage Dip

1 pound ground sausage

2 (8 ounce) packages cream cheese

1 (8 ounce) can diced tomatoes with
  chilies

Brown sausage on moderate heat. Drain. In medium bowl, combine sausage, cream cheese, and tomatoes. Place in microwave. In 2-minute intervals, melt and blend mixture until smooth and creamy. Serve with crackers.

YIELD: 8 SERVINGS

Christmas Eve Shrimp Dip

* · * · * · * · *

1 (8 ounce) package cream cheese

1 cup mayonnaise

8 ounces extra-small frozen shrimp, thawed and dried

1 cup chopped green onion

1 cup chopped celery

1 (12 ounce) bag corn chips

Mix cream cheese and mayonnaise until smooth. Add shrimp, onion, and celery. Blend well. Refrigerate until ready to serve with chips.

YIELD: 3 CUPS

Pumpkin Cheesecake Dip

✳ · ✳ · ✳ · ✳ · ✳

1 (8 ounce) package cream cheese, softened

1 (16 ounce) can pumpkin pie filling

2 cups powdered sugar

½ teaspoon cinnamon

½ teaspoon ground ginger

1 (9½ ounce) package gingersnap cookies

In medium bowl, whip cream cheese with hand mixer until smooth. Add pie filling and mix well. Stir in powdered sugar, cinnamon, and ginger. Mix until smooth. Refrigerate mixture for at least 2 hours. Serve with gingersnap cookies.

YIELD: 3 CUPS

Cheesy Reindeer Squares

❄ · ❄ · ❄ · ❄ · ❄

4 cups grated cheddar cheese

1 teaspoon chopped onion

4 eggs, beaten

1 (4 ounce) can chopped green chilies, drained

Preheat oven to 350 degrees. Combine cheese, onion, eggs, and chilies. Mix well. Pour into ungreased 8-inch baking pan. Bake for 30 minutes. Cut into small squares.

YIELD: 10 SERVINGS

Olive Nut Spread

6 ounces cream cheese, softened

½ cup mayonnaise

2 tablespoons olive juice

⅛ teaspoon black pepper

½ cup chopped pecans

1 cup salad olives, drained

35 to 40 small cocktail crackers

Combine cream cheese, mayonnaise, olive juice, pepper, pecans, and olives. Mix well. Refrigerate until ready to serve with crackers.

YIELD: 12 SERVINGS

Crab Melts

1 (6 ounce) can crabmeat

1 (5 ounce) jar cheese spread

½ cup butter, softened

2 tablespoons mayonnaise

¼ teaspoon salt

¼ teaspoon garlic powder

6 English muffins split in half

Combine crabmeat, cheese spread, butter, mayonnaise, salt, and garlic powder. Blend well. Lightly toast muffins and spread with crab mixture. Cut each into 4 pieces and serve.

YIELD: 24 SERVINGS

Three-Cheese Cheesy Balls

✳ · ✳ · ✳ · ✳ · ✳

2 pounds processed cheese

1 pound cheddar cheese

1 pound sharp cheddar cheese

1 cup chopped pecans

Let cheeses stand at room temperature until soft. In large bowl, mix cheeses together with electric mixer until well blended. Chill until firm enough to roll into balls. Form tablespoon-size balls. Roll in pecans.

Yield: 24 servings

Tomato Bacon Cups

8 slices bacon, fried crispy and crumbled

1 medium tomato, finely chopped

¼ cup chopped onion

¼ cup shredded swiss cheese

½ cup mayonnaise

1 teaspoon dried or fresh basil

1 (10 count) tube refrigerated biscuits

Preheat oven to 350 degrees. Combine bacon, tomato, onion, cheese, mayonnaise, and basil. Blend well. Divide each biscuit into 3 pieces and place in greased mini-muffin cups (forming the biscuit pieces into a cup). Place a small amount of mixture onto each biscuit. Bake for 15 minutes.

Yield: 30 servings

Black Bean Dip

2 (12 ounce) cans black beans

1 (12 ounce) can whole kernel corn

1 medium purple onion, finely chopped

4 tablespoons olive oil

4 tablespoons red wine vinegar

¼ cup fresh chopped cilantro

2 tablespoons lime juice

¼ teaspoon salt

¼ teaspoon pepper

Drain beans and corn and pour into large bowl. Add onion, oil, vinegar, cilantro, lime juice, salt, and pepper. Mix well. Refrigerate until ready to serve.

Yield: 12 servings

Cranberry Smoky Snacks

1 (16 ounce) can cranberry sauce

2 (16 count) packages small link sausages, cooked

In large saucepan, melt cranberry sauce over medium heat. Add sausages and heat thoroughly. Keep warm in small Crock-Pot or chafing dish.

Yield: 32 servings

Santa's Sausage Balls and Dipping Sauce

❄ · ❄ · · · ❄ · · ❄

1 pound sausage, uncooked

1 (8 ounce) package cream cheese, softened

1¼ cups prepared biscuit mix

4 ounces cheddar cheese, grated

½ cup mayonnaise

½ cup sour cream

2 tablespoons Dijon mustard

1 tablespoon white wine vinegar

3 drops hot sauce

1 medium garlic clove, crushed

Preheat oven to 400 degrees. Mix together sausage, cream cheese, biscuit mix, and cheese. Blend well and roll into 1-inch balls. Bake for 20 to 25 minutes or until golden brown. To prepare sauce, combine mayonnaise, sour cream, mustard, vinegar, hot sauce, and garlic in medium bowl. Stir until smooth. Refrigerate sauce until ready to serve.

YIELD: 12 SERVINGS

Festive Vegetable Dip

❄ · ❄ · · · ❄ · · ❄

1 cup sour cream

1 cup mayonnaise

½ cup Italian dressing

¼ cup finely chopped red pepper

¼ cup finely chopped green pepper

35 to 40 small cocktail crackers

In small bowl, combine sour cream, mayonnaise, and Italian dressing. Blend well. Add red and green peppers. Stir well. Refrigerate until ready to serve with crackers.

YIELD: 2 CUPS

Recipe:...

INGREDIENTS:..

....

....

DIRECTIONS:...

....

....

....

....

YIELD:..

Recipe:...

INGREDIENTS:..

....

....

DIRECTIONS:...

....

....

....

YIELD:..

Recipe: ....

Ingredients: ....

....

....

Directions: ....

....

....

....

....

Yield: ....

Recipe: ....

Ingredients: ....

....

....

Directions: ....

....

....

....

....

Yield: ....

Recipe: ....

Ingredients: ....

....

....

Directions: ....

....

....

....

....

Yield: ....

On the second day of Christmas my true love sent to me. . .

Two Beverages a-Blending

For centuries men have kept an appointment
with Christmas. Christmas means fellowship, feasting,
giving and receiving, a time of good cheer, home.

W. J. RONALD TUCKER

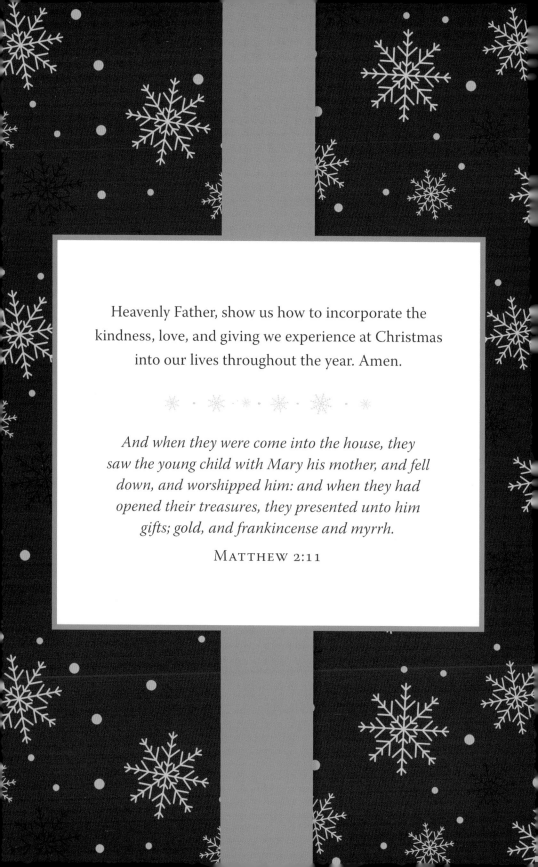

Heavenly Father, show us how to incorporate the kindness, love, and giving we experience at Christmas into our lives throughout the year. Amen.

* · * · * · * · *

And when they were come into the house, they saw the young child with Mary his mother, and fell down, and worshipped him: and when they had opened their treasures, they presented unto him gifts; gold, and frankincense and myrrh.

MATTHEW 2:11

Minty Christmas Creams

✳ · ✳ · ✳ · ✳ · ✳

2 cups crushed ice

2 ounces crème de menthe

4 ounces crème de cacao

6 generous scoops vanilla ice cream

Process ice, crèmes, and ice cream in blender until well mixed. Serve in 2- to 3-ounce glasses.

Yield: 4 cups

Apple Kringle

3 (3 inch) cinnamon sticks, broken into pieces

2 teaspoons whole cloves

2 quarts apple cider

2 cups orange juice

½ cup lemon juice

1 cup sugar

½ teaspoon ground nutmeg

Place cinnamon sticks and cloves in a large tea ball; set aside. Gradually add apple cider, orange juice, and lemon juice to a large pot, stirring well. Add sugar and nutmeg. Add tea ball. Bring mixture to boil. Reduce heat and simmer for 15 minutes. Remove tea ball. Serve warm.

YIELD: 2½ QUARTS

Peppermint Mocha Sodas

2 cups chocolate syrup

8 cups club soda or ginger ale, chilled

1 quart peppermint stick ice cream

1 cup whipped cream

8 maraschino cherries

Set out 8 tall soda glasses on countertop. In each glass, place 3 tablespoons chocolate syrup. Fill glasses half full with club soda or ginger ale. Add 2 scoops ice cream and stir gently. Garnish with whipped cream and cherries.

YIELD: 8 SERVINGS

Sparkling Cider

2 quarts apple cider, chilled

1 cup lemon juice

½ cup sugar

1 (32 ounce) bottle ginger ale, chilled

Apple slices or cinnamon sticks

Ice

Combine cider, lemon juice, and sugar. Stir until sugar is dissolved. When ready to serve, add ginger ale. Garnish with apple slices or cinnamon sticks. Serve over ice.

YIELD: 3 QUARTS

Mint Sparkle

1 (10 ounce) jar mint jelly

1 cup water

2 (12 ounce) cans unsweetened
pineapple juice

1 cup water

½ cup lemon juice

1 (12 ounce) bottle ginger ale,
chilled

Combine jelly with water in medium saucepan. Cook over low heat, stirring constantly, until jelly melts. Cool. Stir in pineapple juice, water, and lemon juice. Chill thoroughly. When ready to serve, add ginger ale.

YIELD: 2 QUARTS

Pineapple Holiday Punch

7 cups pineapple juice, chilled

1 pint orange sherbet

1½ pints vanilla ice cream

3 cups ginger ale, chilled

In large bowl, combine pineapple juice, sherbet, and ice cream. With an electric mixer, blend together until smooth. Refrigerate until ready to serve. Pour into punch bowl. Add ginger ale, stirring gently.

YIELD: 24 CUPS

Fabulous Fruity Punch

✳ · ✳ · ✳ · ✳ · ✳ · ✳

4 cups cranberry juice, chilled

3 cups pineapple juice, chilled

3 cups orange juice, chilled

3 cups club soda, chilled

3 tablespoons lime juice concentrate

Ice ring or cubes

In large punch bowl, combine cranberry, pineapple, and orange juices. Add club soda and lime juice concentrate and blend well. Add ice ring or ice cubes.

YIELD: 16 SERVINGS

Coffee Lover's Holiday Delight

❄ · ❄ · ❄ · ❄ · ❄ · ❄

1 gallon strong coffee, hot

2 cups sugar

1 pint whipping cream (not whipped)

1 gallon vanilla ice cream, softened

Combine coffee and sugar while coffee is hot. Cool completely. Add whipping cream. Place in refrigerator and chill overnight. When ready to serve, add ice cream. Blend well.

Yield: 24 servings

Non-alcoholic Champagne Punch

✳ · ❄ · ✳ · ❄ · ✳

5 cups sugar

2½ cups water, divided

1 tablespoon Fruit Fresh

½ cup lemon juice

2 teaspoons vanilla

2 teaspoons almond extract

6 quarts ginger ale

Mix sugar and 2 cups water in large saucepan. Cook on medium heat until sugar is dissolved. Cool. Dissolve Fruit Fresh in ½ cup water. Add to sugar mixture. Mix well. Add lemon juice, vanilla, and almond extract. Chill. When ready to serve, add 2 quarts ginger ale to each cup of base.

YIELD: 90 SERVINGS

North Pole Wassail

✳ · ❄ · ✳ · ❄ · ✳

1 (12 ounce) can frozen apple juice concentrate

6 cups water

1 (32 ounce) can unsweetened pineapple juice

2 cups orange juice

Juice of 2 lemons

2 cinnamon sticks

6 to 8 whole cloves

In large cooking pot, combine apple juice concentrate and water until blended. Add pineapple juice, orange juice, and lemon juice. Place spices in cheesecloth and tie. Drop into pot and simmer 20 minutes. Remove and discard spices; serve wassail hot.

YIELD: 12 TO 15 SERVINGS

Almond Tea

* · * · * · * · *

3 cups water

3 family-size tea bags

6 cups water

2 cups sugar

1 cup lemon juice

2 teaspoons vanilla

3 teaspoons almond extract

Bring water to boil in teapot or small saucepan. Add tea bags. Steep for 4 minutes. Remove and discard tea bags; set tea aside. In medium saucepan, boil 6 cups water with sugar for 5 minutes. Pour tea into sugar/water mixture. Add lemon juice, vanilla, and almond extract. Chill and serve over ice.

YIELD: 12 TO 15 SERVINGS

· ·

Red Stocking Punch

* · * · * · * · * · *

2 (2 liter) bottles strawberry-flavored red soda

2 (12 ounce) cans lemonade concentrate

1 (2 liter) bottle ginger ale

When ready to serve, combine red soda, lemonade concentrate, and ginger ale in large punch bowl. Stir until well blended.

YIELD: 20 TO 25 SERVINGS

Tomato Cocktail

* · ❋ · * · ❋ · * · ❋ · * · ❋ · * · *

1 quart tomato juice

¼ cup lemon juice

¼ cup lime juice

1 teaspoon Worcestershire sauce

1 (12 ounce) can lemon lime soda

In 1½-quart pitcher, combine juices, Worcestershire sauce, and soda. Stir until well blended. Chill until ready to serve.

Yield: 12 servings

Strawberry Punch

1 (6 ounce) can frozen orange juice concentrate

1 (2 ounce) can frozen lemonade concentrate

1 (16 ounce) container frozen sweetened whole strawberries

6 cups cold water

12 ice cubes

2 (12 ounce) bottles club soda

Slightly defrost concentrates and strawberries. Drain strawberry juice into large punch bowl; set whole berries aside. Add orange juice and lemonade concentrates to punch bowl and stir well. Add 6 cups cold water and ice. Mix well. Add club soda and strawberries. Stir.

YIELD: 3 QUARTS

Banana Christmas Crush

4 cups sugar

1 cup water

1 (46 ounce) can pineapple juice

2 (12 ounce) cans frozen orange juice concentrate, thawed

1 (12 ounce) can frozen lemonade concentrate, thawed

6 bananas, mashed

3 (2 liter) bottles lemon lime soda

In large bowl, dissolve sugar in water. Add pineapple juice, concentrates, and mashed bananas. Blend well. Refrigerate. Just before serving, add lemon lime soda and stir until slushy.

YIELD: 20 TO 25 SERVINGS

Holiday Blackberry Cordial

✻ · ✻ · ✻ · ✻ · ✻

1 quart blackberries

4 cups water

2 cups sugar

2 teaspoons cinnamon

1 teaspoon allspice

1 teaspoon cloves

In saucepan, combine berries and water. Boil for 3 to 5 minutes. Strain; discard berries. Measure juice and return to saucepan. Add 1 cup sugar for 2 cups juice. Add spices. Bring to slow boil. Cook until thick. Pour into bottle. Refrigerate. To serve, pour over ice, or add to water, milk, or tea.

YIELD: 20 SERVINGS

Cinnamon Perked Cider

10 cups apple cider

½ cup cinnamon red hot candies

Pour apple cider into percolator. Place candies in the percolator basket. Cover and perk. Serve hot.

YIELD: 10 SERVINGS

Spiced Cocoa Mix

¼ cup unsweetened cocoa

¾ cup sugar

1 teaspoon cinnamon

⅛ teaspoon allspice

2 cups dry milk powder

Combine cocoa, sugar, and spices. Mix well. Add milk powder and stir until well blended. For each cup combine 2 tablespoons mix with ¼ cup boiling water. Store dry mix in covered 1-quart container.

YIELD: 3 CUPS MIX

The Klaus's Hot Chocolate for Two

1 ounce melting chocolate

4 teaspoons sugar

1 cup boiling water

1 cup milk

In small saucepan, combine chocolate, sugar, and water. Over moderate heat, cook until chocolate is melted and mixture is smooth. Heat milk in microwave for 30 seconds. Add to mixture. Stir and serve.

YIELD: 2 SERVINGS

Bulgarian Christmas Tea

6 lemons

1 gallon brewed tea

2 cups sugar

1 pint water

1 bottle maraschino cherries with juice

1 can pineapple chunks, drained

Slice lemons; remove rinds but do not discard. Add lemon slices to brewed tea; set aside. In small saucepan, combine lemon rinds, sugar, and 1 pint water. Boil until mixture becomes syrupy. Pour into tea. Add cherries and pineapple chunks. Stir well. Serve over ice.

YIELD: 16 SERVINGS

My Favorite Christmas Beverage Recipes

Recipe:..

INGREDIENTS:...

....

....

....

DIRECTIONS:...

....

....

....

....

YIELD:...

Recipe:..

INGREDIENTS:...

....

....

DIRECTIONS:...

....

....

....

YIELD:...

Recipe:

Ingredients:

Directions:

Yield:

Recipe:

Ingredients:

Directions:

Yield:

Recipe:

Ingredients:

Directions:

Yield:

On the third day of Christmas my true love sent to me. . .

Three Breads a-Rising

I wish we could put up some
of the Christmas spirit in jars and
open a jar of it every month.

HARLAN MILLER

Lord Jesus, You came as Mary's little baby and became our risen Lord. Send Your peace to rest on us as we serve You during this Christmas season. Amen.

*　·　*　·　*　·　*　·　*

And Mary said, Behold the handmaid of the Lord; be it unto me according to thy word. And the angel departed from her.

LUKE 1:38

Walnut Streusel Muffins

2 cups flour

1½ cups brown sugar

¾ cup butter, softened

¾ cup chopped walnuts, divided

1 cup flour

2 teaspoons baking powder

½ teaspoon baking soda

½ teaspoon salt

1 teaspoon nutmeg

1 teaspoon cinnamon

¼ teaspoon ginger

1 cup buttermilk

2 eggs, beaten

Preheat oven to 350 degrees. Mix together flour, sugar, and butter until blended. Combine ¾ cup of these crumbs with ¼ cup chopped walnuts. Set aside. In large bowl, combine remaining crumb mixture, remaining walnuts, flour, baking powder, baking soda, salt, spices, buttermilk, and eggs. Mix well. Spoon into 12 paper-lined muffin cups, filling ⅔ full. Top each with a spoonful of the reserved crumbs. Bake for 20 minutes.

YIELD: 1 DOZEN MUFFINS

Banana Peanut Bread

1½ cups flour

2 teaspoons baking powder

½ teaspoon baking soda

½ teaspoon salt

1 cup bran

½ cup chopped peanuts

2½ cups mashed bananas

2 tablespoons water

¼ cup shortening

½ cup sugar

1 egg

1 teaspoon vanilla

Preheat oven to 350 degrees. Combine flour, baking powder, baking soda, and salt. Stir in bran and peanuts. Set aside. In measuring cup, combine bananas and water and mix well. Set aside. In large bowl, cream shortening until soft. Add sugar, egg, and vanilla. Beat until light and fluffy. Add dry ingredients alternately with banana mixture, stirring well after each addition. Pour into greased 9x5-inch loaf pan and bake for 40 to 50 minutes. Cool before cutting.

Yield: 1 loaf

Nutty Pumpkin Bread

※ · ※ · ※ · ※ · ※ · ※

3½ cups flour

2 teaspoons salt

1 teaspoon nutmeg

1 teaspoon cinnamon

3 cups sugar

2 teaspoons baking soda

2 cups canned pumpkin

4 eggs, beaten

½ cup vegetable oil

½ cup melted butter

1 cup milk

Preheat oven to 350 degrees. In large bowl, combine flour, salt, spices, sugar, and baking soda. Separately, beat together pumpkin, eggs, oil, butter, and milk. Blend both mixtures together thoroughly and pour into 3 greased and floured 9x5-inch loaf pans, filling each ⅔ full. Bake for 50 to 60 minutes. When knife inserted into middle comes out clean, bread is done.

YIELD: 3 LOAVES

Oatmeal Banana Muffins

※ · ※ · ※ · ※ · ※ · ※

½ cup butter, softened

2 eggs

1 cup mashed bananas

½ cup honey

⅓ cup plain yogurt

1 teaspoon baking soda

1½ cups white or wheat flour

1 cup rolled oats

Preheat oven to 375 degrees. In large bowl, combine butter, eggs, bananas, honey, and yogurt. Add baking soda and mix well. Add flour in portions, mixing just until blended. Stir in oats. Pour into greased muffin cups until ⅔ full. Bake for 18 to 20 minutes. Remove from pans and cool on wire rack.

YIELD: 18 MUFFINS

Frosty Pumpkin Donuts

3 cups flour

¾ teaspoon cinnamon

½ teaspoon nutmeg

1¼ teaspoons salt

¾ teaspoon cream of tartar

2 tablespoons shortening

¾ cup brown sugar, firmly packed

2 eggs and 1 egg yolk

1 cup canned pumpkin

¼ cup sour milk

2 cups vegetable oil for frying

Granulated sugar

Sift together flour, spices, salt, and cream of tartar. Set aside. In large bowl, cream shortening and brown sugar. Add eggs. Mix well. Add pumpkin. Mix well. Add sour milk. Mix well. Add dry ingredients to pumpkin mixture and stir until smooth. Handling as little as possible, roll dough on floured board to ⅜-inch thickness. Let stand for 20 minutes. Cut with a 2½-inch donut cutter. Heat oil to 360 degrees. Fry donuts until brown, turning when first crack appears. Drain on paper towel–lined cookie sheet. When cool, shake donuts in a bag of granulated sugar.

YIELD: 10 TO 12 DONUTS

Orange Nut Bread

2¾ cups flour

2½ teaspoons baking powder

½ teaspoon baking soda

½ teaspoon salt

2 tablespoons butter, softened

1 cup honey

1 egg, beaten

1 tablespoon orange zest

¾ cup orange juice

¾ cup chopped nuts

1 (8 ounce) package cream cheese

Preheat oven to 325 degrees. Sift together flour, baking powder, baking soda, and salt. Set aside. In large bowl, blend together butter and honey. In separate bowl, combine egg and orange zest. Add to butter mixture and mix well. Add dry ingredients alternately with orange juice, mixing well after each addition. Add nuts and stir. Pour into greased 9x5-inch loaf pan. Bake for 1 hour and 10 minutes. Serve warm with cream cheese.

YIELD: 1 LARGE LOAF

Holiday Fruit Loaf

2 cups flour

1 cup sugar

2 teaspoons baking powder

½ teaspoon salt

1 teaspoon orange peel, finely shredded

2 eggs

½ cup milk

½ cup butter, melted

¾ cup fresh cranberries, chopped

¾ cup walnuts, toasted and chopped

½ cup dried figs or dates, chopped

Preheat oven to 350 degrees. In large bowl, stir together flour, sugar, baking powder, and salt. Stir in orange peel. Make well in center of flour. Set aside. Whisk together eggs, milk, and butter. Add to well in flour mixture. Stir until moistened. Batter will be lumpy. Stir in cranberries, walnuts, and figs or dates. Spoon batter into greased 8x4x2-inch loaf pan. Spread evenly. Bake for 65 minutes. Cool for 10 minutes. Remove from pan. Cool completely. Wrap and store overnight before slicing.

YIELD: 12 TO 14 SERVINGS

Jolly Squash Rolls

1 cup milk

2 tablespoons sugar

1¼ teaspoons salt

2 tablespoons shortening

1 package dry yeast

¾ cup mashed, cooked winter squash

3½ to 4 cups flour, sifted

2 tablespoons butter, melted

Preheat oven to 450 degrees. Over low heat, stir together milk, sugar, salt, and shortening until melted. Cool to lukewarm. Stir in yeast and squash. Stir in enough flour to make a soft dough. Place in greased bowl and turn once to oil all sides. Cover with towel. Let rise until double in bulk. Punch down and cover again. Let rise until double. Pull off pieces of dough and roll into balls. Place on greased cookie sheet, close enough to touch. Cover with damp cloth and let rise in a warm spot until double. Bake for 12 minutes. Remove from oven and brush with butter.

YIELD: 18 ROLLS

Soda Bread

1½ cups ginger ale

2 tablespoons sugar

3 cups self-rising flour

Preheat oven to 350 degrees. Slowly mix together ginger ale, sugar, and flour. Pour into well-greased, 9x5-inch loaf pan. Bake for 45 minutes. Serve with honey butter or apple butter.

YIELD: 8 SERVINGS

Sweet Potato Biscuits

1 cup flour

1 tablespoon baking powder

½ teaspoon salt

3 tablespoons butter

1 cup cooked, mashed sweet potatoes

¼ cup milk

Preheat oven to 450 degrees. Combine flour, baking powder, and salt. Cut in butter. Add sweet potatoes and mix well. Gradually add milk to make a soft dough. Turn dough onto floured surface and knead lightly. Roll dough to ⅓-inch thickness. Cut into rounds with a 2-inch biscuit cutter. Place on baking sheet. Bake for 12 to 15 minutes.

YIELD: 12 BISCUITS

Festive Onion Cheese Loaf

1 cup chopped onion

1 tablespoon shortening

1 egg, slightly beaten

½ cup milk

1½ cups biscuit baking mix

1 cup sharp cheddar cheese

1 tablespoon poppy seeds

2 tablespoons melted butter

Preheat oven to 400 degrees. Sauté onion in shortening until golden. In small bowl, beat egg and milk. Place biscuit mix in large bowl. Add egg mixture. Blend well. Add onion and half the cheese. Spread dough into well-greased 8x1-inch round glass baking dish. Sprinkle top with remaining cheese and poppy seeds. Drizzle melted butter over all. Bake for 25 minutes.

YIELD: 6 TO 8 SERVINGS

Garlic Cheese Biscuits

✳ · ❄ · ✳ · ❄ · ✳ · ❄ · ✳

1¼ cups biscuit baking mix

½ cup grated cheddar cheese

⅓ cup water

¼ cup butter, melted

¼ teaspoon garlic powder

¼ teaspoon salt

⅛ teaspoon dried parsley flakes

Preheat oven to 425 degrees. In small bowl, combine biscuit mix and cheese. Add water and stir until mixed well. Drop dough by tablespoon onto well-greased baking sheet. Bake for 10 minutes. While baking, mix together butter, garlic powder, salt, and parsley flakes. Brush or spoon over biscuits after removed from oven.

Yield: 8 biscuits

Butterlove Rolls

1 package yeast

½ cup warm water

½ cup scalded milk

1 egg, beaten

1 teaspoon salt

½ cup sugar

2½ cups flour

¼ cup butter, melted

Preheat oven to 400 degrees. Dissolve yeast in water; set aside. In saucepan, scald milk. Cool in large bowl. Add egg, salt, and sugar. Mix well. Add flour. Mix and knead gently. Let rise until double in size. Roll out in two circles and brush with half the butter. Cut into pie-shaped wedges and roll up crescent-roll style. Brush with remaining butter. Let rise. Bake for 15 minutes or until golden brown.

YIELD: 12 SERVINGS

Parmesan Sticks

1 egg, well beaten

½ cup milk

9 slices white bread, crusts removed

½ cup butter, melted

1½ cups freshly grated Parmesan cheese

Preheat oven to 350 degrees. In small bowl, beat egg and milk together. Soak 3 slices of bread in mixture. Place each soaked bread slice between 2 slices of bread. Press gently until the three slices stick together. Cut each into 4 strips. Roll each strip in butter and then Parmesan cheese. Place on baking sheet and chill for at least 4 hours. Just before serving, place on ungreased baking sheet. Bake for 10 minutes.

YIELD: 12 SERVINGS

Sour Cream Biscuits

1 cup butter, softened

1 (8 ounce) carton sour cream

2 cups self-rising flour

Preheat oven to 400 degrees. Cream butter. Add sour cream and flour, mixing well with fork. Drop into greased mini-muffin pans. Bake for 15 minutes or until golden brown.

YIELD: 24 SERVINGS

Herb Toast

1 cup butter, melted

1 (.4 ounce) garlic and herb salad
dressing mix

1 teaspoon dried dill weed

¼ teaspoon salt

20 thin slices bread

Preheat oven to 300 degrees. In small bowl, combine butter, dressing mix, dill weed, and salt. Trim crusts from bread. Flatten each slice with rolling pin and roll tightly. Coat each slice with butter mixture. Place on ungreased baking sheet and bake for 18 minutes.

YIELD: 20 SERVINGS

Happy Hush Puppies

2 cups self-rising cornmeal

½ cup finely chopped onion

1 teaspoon salt

1 teaspoon cayenne pepper

1½ cups boiling water

Vegetable oil for frying

Combine cornmeal, onion, salt, and cayenne pepper. Stir in boiling water and mix well. Heat oil to 360 degrees. Drop dough by rounded tablespoon into hot oil. Fry 1 minute, then flip and fry another minute or until lightly browned on both sides. Drain well.

YIELD: 24 SERVINGS

Holiday Honey Bread

1 package yeast

¼ cup warm water

1 cup hot water

½ cup butter

¼ cup honey

1 teaspoon salt

3¼ cups sifted flour, divided

2 eggs

1 cup oatmeal

Preheat oven to 350 degrees. Soften yeast in ¼ cup water; set aside. In large bowl, blend 1 cup hot water, butter, honey, and salt. Cool to lukewarm. Stir in 1½ cups flour and beat until smooth. Blend in yeast, eggs, and oatmeal. Add remaining flour and beat until smooth. Cover and let rise in warm place for 1 hour. Punch down and lightly knead. Turn into 2-quart round casserole dish. Bake for 60 minutes. Allow to stand for 10 minutes before removing from dish.

Yield: 8 to 10 servings

Easy Spoon Rolls

1 package dry yeast

2 cups warm water

1 egg

4 cups self-rising flour

½ cup sugar

¾ cup shortening, melted

Preheat oven to 425 degrees. Dissolve yeast in warm water. Add egg, flour, sugar, and shortening. Blend well. Spoon into greased muffin pans. Bake for 20 minutes.

YIELD: 12 SERVINGS

French Cheese Bread

1 loaf garlic french bread, sliced in half lengthwise

¾ cup mayonnaise

1 cup grated cheddar cheese

Preheat oven to 400 degrees. Spread mayonnaise over flat tops of bread. Sprinkle grated cheddar cheese over all. Bake for 20 minutes until cheese bubbles and turns slightly brown.

YIELD: 10 TO 12 SERVINGS

Recipe:

INGREDIENTS:

DIRECTIONS:

YIELD:

Recipe:

INGREDIENTS:

DIRECTIONS:

YIELD:

Recipe: ....

INGREDIENTS: ....

....

....

DIRECTIONS: ....

....

....

....

....

YIELD: ....

Recipe: ....

INGREDIENTS: ....

....

....

DIRECTIONS: ....

....

....

....

YIELD: ....

Recipe: ....

INGREDIENTS: ....

....

....

DIRECTIONS: ....

....

....

....

YIELD: ....

On the fourth day of Christmas my true love sent to me...

Four Breakfast Dishes a-Baking

What is Christmas?
It is tenderness for the past,
courage for the present,
hope for the future.

AGNES M. PHARO

Father in heaven, thank You for the gifts You pour
out on us each Christmas—gifts of incalculable value. . .
gifts of peace, joy, kindness, and love. Amen.

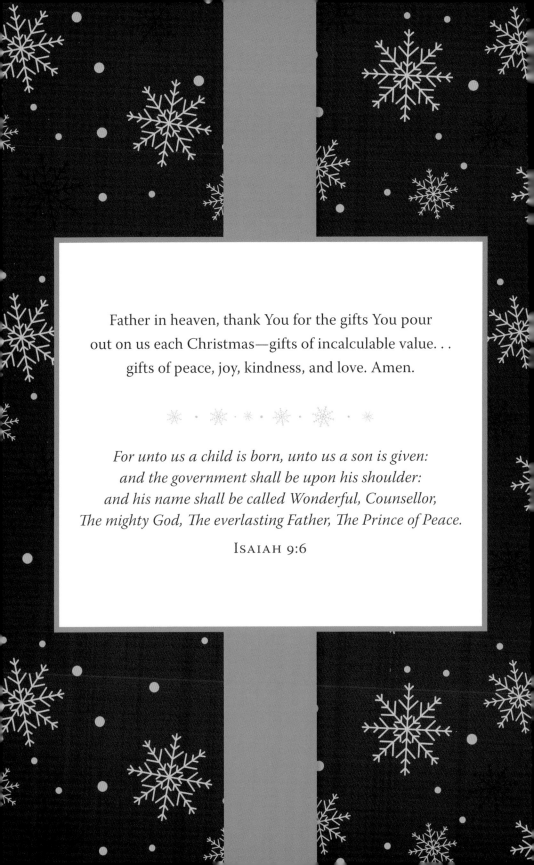

For unto us a child is born, unto us a son is given:
and the government shall be upon his shoulder:
and his name shall be called Wonderful, Counsellor,
The mighty God, The everlasting Father, The Prince of Peace.

Isaiah 9:6

Christmas Morning Coffee Cake

✳ · ✳ · ✳ · ✳ · ✳

2 cups biscuit mix

⅔ cup milk

½ cup rolled oats, uncooked

1 egg

2 tablespoons firmly packed
  brown sugar

½ teaspoon cinnamon

⅔ cup rolled oats, uncooked

⅔ cup firmly packed brown sugar

½ cup chopped nuts

¼ cup butter, melted

½ teaspoon cinnamon

Preheat oven to 375 degrees. In large bowl, combine biscuit mix, milk, ½ cup oats, egg, brown sugar, and cinnamon. Blend well. Spread half the batter in greased 8-inch square pan. In another bowl, combine ⅔ cup oats, brown sugar, nuts, butter, and cinnamon. Sprinkle half the topping over the cake batter. Pour remaining batter into pan. Then sprinkle remaining topping over batter. Bake for 40 minutes. Serve warm.

Yield: 9 servings

Broccoli Bacon Quiche

4 eggs

1 cup half-and-half

1 cup grated swiss cheese

2 cups broccoli flowerets

¼ teaspoon salt

⅛ teaspoon garlic powder

⅛ teaspoon lemon pepper

2 slices bacon, cooked until crisp and crumbled

Preheat oven to 350 degrees. Beat eggs with half-and-half and cheese. Stir in broccoli, salt, garlic powder, and lemon pepper. Stir half the bacon into egg mixture. Pour mixture into 9-inch pie plate. Bake for 30 to 35 minutes. Top with remaining bacon before serving.

YIELD: 4 SERVINGS

Welsh Rarebit

1 egg, beaten

1 teaspoon Worcestershire sauce

½ teaspoon salt

¼ teaspoon cayenne pepper

1 teaspoon mustard

¾ cup scalded milk

2 cups shredded sharp cheddar cheese

4 English muffins, toasted and buttered

In small bowl, combine egg, Worcestershire sauce, salt, cayenne pepper, and mustard; set aside. In heavy saucepan, scald milk. Add cheese and stir until melted. Add egg mixture and stir over low heat until thickened. Just before serving, pour over English muffins.

YIELD: 4 SERVINGS

Cinnamon Raisin French Toast

✳ · ✳ · ✳ · ✳ · ✳ · ✳

6 large eggs

½ cup heavy cream

1 teaspoon cinnamon

½ teaspoon salt

1 tablespoon butter

1 (12 ounce) loaf unsliced raisin bread

1 cup whipped cream or maple syrup

In large bowl, beat together eggs and cream until blended. Add cinnamon and salt. Mix well; set aside. Melt butter in frying pan. While heating, cut loaf into 2-inch slices. Dip each slice in egg mixture until saturated. Remove before bread becomes soggy. Place immediately in hot butter. Brown on one side. Flip and brown on the other side. Serve with whipped cream or syrup.

YIELD: 6 SERVINGS

Cheesy Christmas Grits

✳ · ✳ · ✳ · ✳ · ✳

4 cups water

1 teaspoon salt

1 cup quick-cooking grits

2 cups grated sharp cheddar cheese

⅔ cup milk

2 tablespoons butter

1 teaspoon Worcestershire sauce

4 eggs, slightly beaten

⅛ teaspoon paprika

Preheat oven to 350 degrees. In large saucepan, bring water, salt, and grits to boil. Cover, reduce heat, and simmer for 5 minutes, stirring occasionally. Remove saucepan from heat. Add cheese, milk, butter, and Worcestershire sauce, stirring until cheese and butter melt. Add eggs and stir. Spoon mixture into casserole dish and sprinkle with paprika. Bake uncovered for 1 hour. Let stand for 5 minutes before cutting.

YIELD: 6 SERVINGS

Fancy Glazed Bacon

* · ❄ · ❄ · ❄ · ❄ · ❄

1 pound bacon

1 cup brown sugar

1 tablespoon Dijon mustard

2 tablespoons red wine

⅛ teaspoon salt

Preheat oven to 350 degrees. Place bacon strips on foil-lined cookie sheet. Bake for 15 minutes or until almost crisp. While bacon is cooking, mix together sugar, mustard, wine, and salt. Drain excess fat from bacon. Pour half the glaze mixture over bacon and return to oven. When well browned, turn bacon over and pour on remaining glaze. Cook another 10 to 15 minutes or until golden brown. Transfer bacon to waxed paper to cool.

YIELD: 6 SERVINGS

Holiday Seafood Quiche

❄ · ❄ · ❄ · ❄ · ❄ · ❄

1 (9 inch) piecrust

6 ounces grated swiss cheese

1 (8 ounce) package imitation crabmeat

½ cup green onion slices

2 tablespoons flour

½ teaspoon salt

⅛ teaspoon pepper

4 eggs

1½ cups half-and-half

Preheat oven to 350 degrees. Roll piecrust into 13-inch circle. Place in 10-inch pie plate. Flute edge. In medium bowl, combine cheese, crabmeat, onion, flour, and seasonings. Pour into piecrust. Beat eggs with half-and-half. Pour over cheese mixture. Bake for 60 minutes.

YIELD: 6 SERVINGS

Overnight Breakfast Rolls

1 (25 ounce) bag frozen
Parker-style rolls

1 (6 ounce) package regular (not
instant) butterscotch pudding

1 cup brown sugar, firmly packed

1 teaspoon cinnamon

½ cup chopped pecans

½ cup butter

Place frozen rolls in ungreased Bundt pan. Pour dry pudding mix and sugar over rolls. Sprinkle cinnamon and nuts over rolls. Cut butter into pieces and place around rolls. Place rolls into cold oven and let rise overnight. Remove from cold oven. Preheat oven to 350 degrees. Bake for 25 minutes. Turn rolls out on foil upside down and serve hot.

YIELD: 12 SERVINGS

Bacon Cheese Breakfast Bake

7 slices white bread, crust removed
and cubed

2 cups grated cheddar cheese

6 eggs

3 cups milk

1 teaspoon ground mustard

½ teaspoon salt

¼ teaspoon pepper

6 bacon strips, cooked
and crumbled

In casserole dish, combine bread cubes and cheese; set aside. In large bowl, whisk together eggs, milk, mustard, salt, and pepper. Pour over bread and cheese. Top with bacon. Cover and refrigerate overnight. Remove from refrigerator 30 minutes before baking. Preheat oven to 350 degrees. Bake uncovered for 55 minutes.

YIELD: 6 SERVINGS

Christmas Morning Puffs

1½ cups flour

1½ teaspoons baking powder

½ teaspoon salt

¼ teaspoon nutmeg

⅓ cup vegetable oil

½ cup sugar

1 egg

½ cup milk

1 teaspoon cinnamon

½ cup sugar

6 tablespoons butter, melted

Preheat oven to 350 degrees. In medium bowl, sift together flour, baking powder, salt, and nutmeg. Set aside. In large bowl, thoroughly combine oil, sugar, and egg. Add dry ingredients alternately with milk, stirring after each addition. Pour into greased muffin cups until ⅔ full. Bake for 20 minutes or until light golden brown. Cool for 3 minutes. Mix together cinnamon and sugar. Loosen muffins with spatula. Dip top and sides in butter. Then roll in cinnamon and sugar mixture. Serve hot.

YIELD: 1 DOZEN

Peach Waffles

⅓ cup shortening

½ cup sugar

2 eggs

2 cups flour

1 tablespoon baking powder

½ teaspoon salt

1 cup milk

1½ cups peeled, diced peaches

½ teaspoon lemon juice

½ teaspoon vanilla

1 tablespoon powdered sugar

In large bowl, cream shortening, gradually adding sugar. Beat well with electric mixer on low speed. Add eggs, one at a time, beating well after each addition. Set aside. In medium bowl, combine flour, baking powder, and salt. Add to creamed mixture alternately with milk. Add peaches, lemon juice, and vanilla. Bake on preheated, oiled waffle iron. Sprinkle with powdered sugar before serving.

YIELD: 16 WAFFLES

Holiday Breakfast Bread

✳ · ✳ · ✳ · ✳ · ✳ · ✳

3 cups flour

2 cups sugar

1 teaspoon salt

1 teaspoon baking soda

1 teaspoon cinnamon

3 eggs, beaten

½ cup oil

1 cup chopped pecans

1 cup coconut flakes

2 cups dried bananas

1 (12 ounce) can crushed pineapple, drained

1½ teaspoons vanilla

Preheat oven to 350 degrees. In large bowl, combine flour, sugar, salt, baking soda, and cinnamon. Mix well. Add eggs and oil. Mix well. Add pecans, coconut, bananas, pineapple, and vanilla. Bake in 2 greased 9x5-inch loaf pans for 1 hour and 20 minutes.

YIELD: 16 SERVINGS

· ·

Deviled Ham Quiche

✳ · ✳ · ✳ · ✳ · ✳ · ✳

1 (9 inch) piecrust

2 eggs, beaten

⅓ cup mayonnaise

⅓ cup evaporated milk

2 tablespoons flour

½ teaspoon mustard

2 tablespoons chopped onion

½ cup shredded cheddar cheese

1 cup shredded swiss cheese

1 (4.25 ounce) can deviled ham

Preheat oven to 325 degrees. Line pie plate with crust and flute edges. In large bowl, combine eggs, mayonnaise, milk, flour, mustard, onion, cheeses, and ham. Pour into piecrust. Bake for 40 minutes.

YIELD: 4 SERVINGS

Serving Santa Breakfast Quiche

½ cup butter

½ cup flour

6 large eggs

2 cups cottage cheese

1 pound Monterrey Jack cheese, cubed

½ teaspoon baking powder

½ teaspoon salt

1 teaspoon sugar

½ cup mushrooms, diced

2 slices bacon, cooked and crumbled

Preheat oven to 350 degrees. Melt butter in small saucepan. Add flour and cook until smooth. Set aside to cool. In large bowl, beat eggs. Add cheeses, baking powder, salt, and sugar. Blend well. Add flour mixture to egg mixture. Stir until well blended. Add mushrooms and bacon. Mix well. Pour into greased 9x12x2-inch baking pan. Bake uncovered for 45 minutes.

YIELD: 8 SERVINGS

Tasty Vidalia Strata

8 slices bread, cubed

2 cups shredded cheddar cheese, divided

2 large Vidalia onions, thinly sliced

2 eggs, beaten

2 cups milk

1½ tablespoons mustard

1 teaspoon salt

¼ teaspoon pepper

¼ teaspoon paprika

Preheat oven to 325 degrees. Place half the bread cubes in greased 2-quart casserole dish. Sprinkle 1 cup cheese over bread. Layer onion slices. Repeat layers of bread, cheese, and onion. Beat together eggs, milk, mustard, salt, and pepper. Pour over top of casserole. Sprinkle with paprika. Bake for 1 hour.

YIELD: 6 SERVINGS

Elegant Shrimp Scramble

3 slices bacon, cooked and crumbled, reserve drippings

¾ cup chopped green pepper

½ cup chopped onion

¼ teaspoon salt

¼ teaspoon cayenne pepper

10 ounces cooked shrimp, coarsely chopped

6 eggs, beaten

¼ cup half-and-half

½ teaspoon Worcestershire sauce

Sauté green pepper and onion in reserved bacon drippings until tender. Add salt and cayenne pepper. Add shrimp. Stir until heated thoroughly. In bowl, combine eggs, half-and-half, Worcestershire sauce, and bacon. Add to shrimp mixture and cook until eggs are firm, stirring occasionally.

YIELD: 6 SERVINGS

Colorful Egg Lover's Casserole

❄ · ❄ · ❄ · ❄ · ❄ · ❄

6 eggs, hard-boiled and finely
    chopped

2 tablespoons chopped pimiento

¼ cup chopped celery

1 cup mayonnaise

1 teaspoon salt

¾ teaspoon garlic salt

¼ teaspoon pepper

¼ cup milk

1½ cups cracker crumbs, divided

2 tablespoons butter, melted

Preheat oven to 400 degrees. In mixing bowl, combine eggs, pimiento, celery, mayonnaise, salt, garlic salt, pepper, and milk. Add 1 cup of cracker crumbs. Spoon into greased 1-quart casserole dish. Combine remaining crumbs and butter. Sprinkle over egg mixture. Bake for 25 minutes or until brown.

Yield: 6 servings

. . . .

Egg Foo Young

❄ · ❄ · ❄ · ❄ · ❄

6 eggs

4 green onions, thinly sliced

¾ cup frozen green peas

1 cup chopped mushrooms

1½ cups bean sprouts

8 to 10 medium shrimp, coarsely
    chopped

1 tablespoon soy sauce

2 tablespoons oil

In large bowl, beat eggs. Add onions, peas, mushrooms, sprouts, shrimp, and soy sauce. Blend well. Heat oil in heavy skillet to medium high. Spoon 2 tablespoons of mixture into skillet for each serving (should spread out like a pancake). When each is set and brown underneath, turn over and brown other side. Serve immediately.

Yield: 6 servings

My Favorite Christmas Breakfast Recipes

Recipe:..
Ingredients:...
....
....
Directions:...
....
....
....
....
Yield:...

Recipe:..
Ingredients:...
....
Directions:...
....
....
....
Yield:...

Recipe:..
INGREDIENTS:..
....
....
DIRECTIONS:...
....
....
....
YIELD:..

Recipe:..
INGREDIENTS:..
....
....
DIRECTIONS:...
....
....
....
YIELD:..

Recipe:..
INGREDIENTS:..
....
....
DIRECTIONS:...
....
....
....
YIELD:..

On the fifth day of Christmas my true love sent to me. . .

Five Candies a-Boiling

Like snowflakes, my Christmas
memories gather and dance—
each beautiful, unique,
and too soon gone.

DEBORAH WHIPP

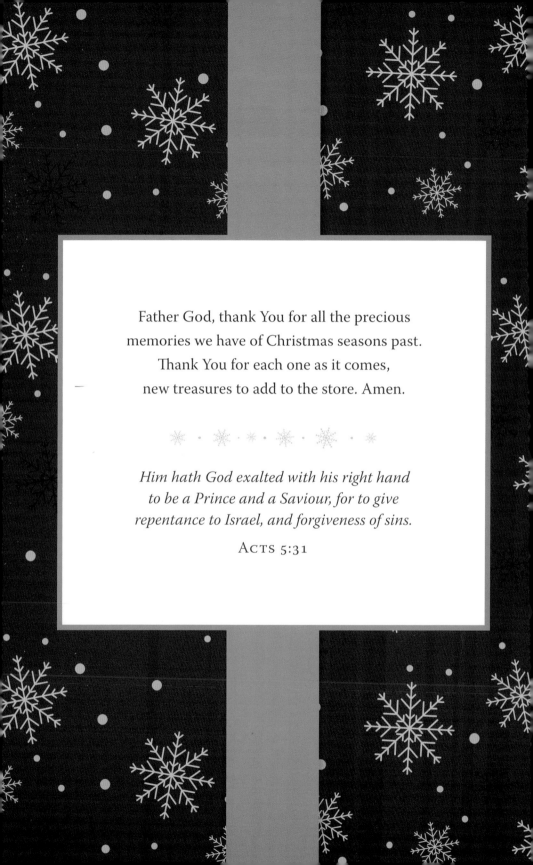

Father God, thank You for all the precious
memories we have of Christmas seasons past.
Thank You for each one as it comes,
new treasures to add to the store. Amen.

*Him hath God exalted with his right hand
to be a Prince and a Saviour, for to give
repentance to Israel, and forgiveness of sins.*

ACTS 5:31

English Toffee

2 cups sugar

1½ cups butter

2 tablespoons water

½ teaspoon salt

½ cup grated milk chocolate

2 cups chopped pecans

In heavy saucepan, combine sugar, butter, water, salt, and chocolate. Cook over low heat until gently boiling. Boil until mixture reaches 260 degrees or hard ball stage. Spread in shallow baking pan and sprinkle nuts on top. Cool and break into pieces.

YIELD: 1 POUND

Pecan Date Roll

3 cups sugar

1 cup whole milk

1 tablespoon butter

½ teaspoon salt

1½ cups pitted and chopped dates

1 teaspoon vanilla

1 cup chopped pecans

½ cup flaked coconut, optional

In heavy saucepan, combine sugar, milk, butter, and salt. Boil until mixture reaches 236 degrees or soft ball stage. Add dates and cook gently for another 3 minutes. Remove from heat and stir in vanilla. Cool mixture in pan until lukewarm. Beat until creamy while adding nuts. Turn out onto flat surface and form into log. Roll in coconut, if desired. Chill covered; cut into slices before serving.

YIELD: 2 DOZEN SLICES

Chocolate Peanut Butter Balls

✳ · ✳ · ✳ · ✳ · ✳

2 cups creamy peanut butter

3 cups sifted powdered sugar

1 (12 ounce) bag milk chocolate chips

⅓ cup white chocolate chips

3 tablespoons butter

2 tablespoons shortening

1 cup peanuts

Cream peanut butter and sugar. Use mixture to form 36 balls. Place on waxed paper and refrigerate for 30 minutes. Melt chips, butter, and shortening in double boiler. Mixture should be thin for dipping. Crush peanuts and set aside. Roll balls in melted chocolate while still over double boiler. Place on wire rack until almost set. Roll in peanuts. Return to refrigerator for 30 minutes before serving.

Yield: 36 balls

Bitter Sweets

½ cup butter, softened

3½ cups powdered sugar

1 tablespoon milk

1 teaspoon vanilla

1 teaspoon salt

1 square bitter chocolate

1 teaspoon shortening

In large bowl, cream butter. Add sugar, milk, vanilla, and salt. Work into dough. Form balls. Chill. Melt chocolate with shortening. Dip balls into chocolate and place on waxed paper to cool.

YIELD: 2 DOZEN

Millionaire Candy

1 pound caramels

1 tablespoon water

3 cups pecans

1 (16 ounce) plain chocolate bar

½ pound paraffin

Combine caramels and water in double boiler and melt. Add pecans and stir. Drop by spoonful onto waxed paper. Chill until firm. In double boiler, melt chocolate bar and paraffin. Dip caramel patties in chocolate. Place on waxed paper until set.

YIELD: 2 DOZEN PIECES

Butter Cream Mints

✳ · ✳ · ✳ · ✳ · ✳

½ cup butter

3½ cups powdered sugar, divided

1 egg, beaten

⅛ teaspoon salt

1 teaspoon pure mint extract

In large bowl, cream butter with half the powdered sugar. Add egg. Mix well. Add remaining sugar, salt, and mint extract. Mixture should be stiff enough to stand without spreading. If too thin, add a little sugar. Using a teaspoon or pastry tube, drop dough onto greased surface or waxed paper. Allow 1 hour to set.

YIELD: 3 DOZEN MINTS

Nut Balls

✳ · ✳ · ✳ · ✳ · ✳

4 cups sugar

1 cup water

2 tablespoons vinegar

⅛ teaspoon baking soda

1 cup flaked coconut

1 cup chopped raisins

1 cup chopped almonds

1 cup chopped pecans

1 (12 ounce) bag chocolate chips

2 tablespoons shortening

In large, heavy saucepan, combine sugar, water, vinegar, and baking soda. Over low heat, cook until well blended and sugar has melted. Increase to moderate heat and boil until mixture reaches 300 degrees or brittle stage. Pour onto greased cookie sheet. Allow to cool enough to pull like taffy until light in color. Work in coconut, raisins, almonds, and pecans. Form balls. Cool slightly. Melt chocolate chips with shortening. Stir well. Cool slightly. Dip balls into chocolate and place on waxed paper until set.

YIELD: 3 DOZEN BALLS

Sour Cream Fudge

✻ · ✻ · ✻ · ✻ · ✻ · ✻

2 cups sugar

1 tablespoon white corn syrup

2 tablespoons butter

1 (12 ounce) carton sour cream

1 teaspoon vanilla

½ cup walnuts

In medium-sized, heavy saucepan, combine sugar, syrup, butter, and sour cream. Blend well. Boil on moderate heat until mixture reaches 238 degrees or soft ball stage. Remove from heat. Add vanilla and nuts. Pour into greased 9x9-inch pan. Cool until set. Cut into squares.

Yield: 9 servings

Martha Washington Candy

2 (1 pound) boxes powdered sugar

1 (12 ounce) can sweetened condensed milk

½ cup butter, melted

8 ounces flaked coconut

2 cups pecans

1 teaspoon vanilla

12 ounces chocolate chips

¼ pound paraffin

In medium bowl, combine powdered sugar, milk, butter, coconut, pecans, and vanilla. Blend well. Chill for 1 hour. Roll into small balls. In double boiler, melt chocolate chips and paraffin. Dip balls into chocolate. Place on waxed paper until set.

Yield: 3 dozen

Jolly Elf Divinity

3 cups sugar

¾ cup light corn syrup

¾ cup water

2 egg whites

1 (3 ounce) box lime or cherry gelatin

½ cup coconut flakes

1 cup chopped pecans or walnuts

In heavy saucepan, combine sugar, corn syrup, and water. Boil until mixture reaches 245 degrees or medium firm ball stage. While mixture is boiling, beat egg whites in bowl until soft peaks form. Add gelatin in small amounts, beating in each portion. Beat until stiff peaks form. When syrup mixture is right consistency, slowly pour over gelatin mixture, beating constantly until mixture stiffens and loses glossy look. Add coconut and nuts. Drop by teaspoonful onto waxed paper.

YIELD: 20 SERVINGS

Nutty Noodle Candy

2 (6 ounce) bags chocolate chips

2 (6 ounce) bags butterscotch chips

1 (3 ounce) can chow mein noodles

½ cup peanuts or pecans

2 cups mini marshmallows

In heavy saucepan, melt chocolate and butterscotch chips, stirring constantly. Remove from heat. Stir in noodles, nuts, and marshmallows. Drop by teaspoonful onto waxed paper. Let set for 1 hour until firm.

YIELD: 12 TO 18 SERVINGS

Christmas White Fudge

❄ · ❄ · ❄ · ❄ · ❄

2 cups sugar

½ cup sour cream

⅓ cup light corn syrup

2 tablespoons butter

¼ teaspoon salt

2 teaspoons vanilla

¼ cup candied cherries, chopped

1 cup chopped pecans

In heavy saucepan, combine sugar, sour cream, corn syrup, butter, and salt. Boil until mixture reaches 238 degrees or soft ball stage. Remove from heat and cool for 15 minutes. Add vanilla and beat until candy is no longer glossy. Add cherries and nuts. Pour into greased 9x13-inch baking pan. Cool and cut into squares.

Yield: 2 dozen squares

Terrific Toffee

2 cups salted butter

2 cups sugar

½ cup chocolate chips

½ cup finely chopped walnuts

Grease large cookie sheet with sides and set aside. In heavy saucepan, melt butter and sugar slowly over medium heat. Boil until mixture reaches 260 degrees or hard crack stage. (Should be color of peanut butter.) Pour into greased cookie sheet. While warm, top with chocolate chips and spread evenly. When chocolate begins to harden, sprinkle with walnuts and press into chocolate with spatula or sheet of waxed paper.

Yield: 2 dozen

Peanut Patties

2½ cups sugar

⅔ cup corn syrup

2½ cups raw peanuts

⅛ teaspoon salt

4 teaspoons butter

Red food coloring

1 cup powdered sugar

1 teaspoon vanilla

In heavy saucepan, boil sugar, corn syrup, peanuts, and salt until mixture reaches 238 degrees or soft ball stage. Stir in butter, a small squirt of food coloring, powdered sugar, and vanilla. Cool slightly. Drop by tablespoonful onto waxed paper.

YIELD: 12 SERVINGS

Date Delight

½ cup butter

1 cup sugar

1 teaspoon vanilla

1 cup pecans

8 ounces pitted dates

2 tablespoons milk

3 cups crispy rice cereal

1 cup flaked coconut

In heavy saucepan, melt butter and sugar over low heat. Stir in vanilla, pecans, dates, milk, and cereal. Cool. Form into balls. Roll in coconut. Place on cookie sheet until set.

YIELD: 2 DOZEN

Peanut Butter Fudge

* · * · * · * · *

2 cups sugar

1 cup milk

1 teaspoon vanilla

1 heaping tablespoon peanut butter

In large skillet, bring sugar, milk, and vanilla to rapid boil. Stir constantly. Boil until mixture reaches 238 degrees or soft ball stage. Add peanut butter. Stir until no longer glossy. Pour into greased 9x9-inch pan. Cool. Cut into squares.

YIELD: 9 SERVINGS

Black Walnut Brittle

1 cup sugar

½ cup light corn syrup

¼ teaspoon salt

¼ cup water

1 cup black walnuts, chopped

2 tablespoons butter, softened

1 teaspoon baking soda

In heavy pan, combine sugar, corn syrup, salt, and water. Over medium heat, bring to boil, stirring until sugar is dissolved. Stir in walnuts and boil, stirring frequently, until mixture reaches 260 degrees or hard crack stage. Remove from heat. Add butter and baking soda. Pour onto greased cookie sheet. When cool, break into pieces.

YIELD: ½ POUND

My Favorite Christmas Candy Recipes

Recipe:..

INGREDIENTS:..

....

....

....

DIRECTIONS:..

....

....

....

....

YIELD:..

Recipe:..

INGREDIENTS:..

....

....

....

DIRECTIONS:..

....

....

....

....

YIELD:..

Recipe:...
INGREDIENTS:...
....
....
DIRECTIONS:..
....
....
....
....

YIELD:...

Recipe:...
INGREDIENTS:...
....
....
DIRECTIONS:..
....
....
....
....

YIELD:...

Recipe:...
INGREDIENTS:...
....
....
DIRECTIONS:..
....
....
....
....

YIELD:...

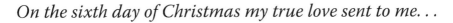

Six Cookies a-Cooling

Perhaps the best Yuletide
decoration is being wreathed in smiles.

Author Unknown

Dear Lord, as we celebrate Your birth,
give us generous, serving hearts that honor
You in everything we say and do. Amen.

*Behold, a virgin shall be with child, and shall bring
forth a son, and they shall call his name Emmanuel,
which being interpreted is, God with us.*

MATTHEW 1:23

Pecan Tessies

✳ · ✳ · ✳ · ✳ · ✳ · ✳

6 ounces cream cheese, softened

1 cup butter, softened

2 cups flour

½ teaspoon salt

2 eggs

1½ cups brown sugar

2 tablespoons butter

2 teaspoons vanilla

1½ cups chopped pecans

Preheat oven to 325 degrees. In medium bowl, cream together cream cheese and butter. Stir in flour and salt. Chill for 1 hour. Press into ungreased mini-muffin pans. Set aside. Cream together eggs, brown sugar, butter, and vanilla. Add nuts and mix well. Pour filling over dough in muffin pans. Bake for 20 minutes.

YIELD: 2 DOZEN

Coconut Delight Bars

✳ · ✳ · ✳ · ✳ · ✳ · ✳

3 cups buttery snack cracker
   crumbs

1½ cups butter

1½ cups whole milk

3 (3 ounce) packages coconut
   instant pudding

½ gallon vanilla ice cream, softened

8 ounces whipped topping

Mix cracker crumbs and butter. Press half the crumb mixture into 9x13-inch pan. In large bowl, mix milk and pudding. Stir in softened ice cream and whipped topping until well blended. Pour over crust and top with remaining crumbs. Chill and serve.

YIELD: 15 BARS

Mexican Holiday Cookies

✳ · ✳ · ✳ · ✳ · ✳ · ✳

2 cups butter

1 cup sugar

1 egg

1 teaspoon vanilla

5 cups flour

1 teaspoon baking soda

½ teaspoon ground cloves

1 teaspoon cinnamon

½ teaspoon ground anise powder

1 teaspoon salt

Juice of one orange (about ¼ cup)

¼ cup sugar

¼ cup cinnamon

Preheat oven to 350 degrees. In large bowl, cream butter, sugar, egg, and vanilla. In separate bowl, combine flour, baking soda, spices, and salt. Mix together with creamed mixture. Stir in orange juice. Roll out dough on floured surface and cut into desired shapes. Bake cookies on ungreased cookie sheet for 8 minutes. Cool just until firm. Combine sugar and cinnamon and dust tops.

YIELD: 3 DOZEN

Santa's Shortbread Cookies

2 cups butter, softened

1 cup sugar

4½ cups flour

sugar

Preheat oven to 275 degrees. In large bowl, cream butter and sugar. Add flour, one cup at a time. Mix thoroughly after each portion. Work dough until easy to handle. On floured board, roll to ½-inch thickness and make a square. Prick top of dough and cut into 1½-inch bars. Place close together on ungreased cookie sheets, baking all at the same time. Bake for 55 minutes or until light brown. While hot, sprinkle lightly with sugar.

YIELD: 4 DOZEN

Butter Pecan Pudding Wonders

1 (18¼ ounce) box butter cake mix

1 (3 ounce) box butter pecan or vanilla instant pudding mix

1 egg

1 cup vegetable oil

1 cup chopped pecans

Preheat oven to 350 degrees. Combine cake mix, pudding mix, egg, and oil. Mix well. Fold in pecans. Roll into small balls. Place on greased cookie sheet. Bake for 10 minutes. Cool slightly and move to rack covered with paper towels. Leave on paper towels for 4 to 6 hours to absorb oil.

YIELD: 15 SERVINGS

Oatmeal Yummies

1 cup shortening

1 cup sugar

1 cup brown sugar

2 eggs, beaten

1 teaspoon vanilla

1 teaspoon salt

1 teaspoon baking soda

3 cups instant or quick oats

1 cup chopped walnuts

Preheat oven to 350 degrees. In large bowl, cream shortening and sugars. Mix in eggs and vanilla. In separate bowl, combine salt and baking soda. Fold into creamed mixture. Stir in oats and nuts. Roll into small balls. Bake for 10 to 12 minutes.

YIELD: 2 DOZEN

Santa's Apple Bars

2 cups sugar

1 cup vegetable oil

3 eggs, beaten

3 cups flour

1 teaspoon baking soda

1 teaspoon salt

1 teaspoon cinnamon

1 cup chopped nuts

3 large red apples with skin, cored
  and diced

2 teaspoons vanilla

Preheat oven to 350 degrees. In large bowl, cream sugar and oil. Add eggs and mix well. In a separate bowl, combine flour, baking soda, salt, and cinnamon. Add to creamed mixture. Fold in nuts, apples, and vanilla. Bake in 9x13-inch greased and floured pan for 30 minutes.

YIELD: 15 BARS

Pecan Sandies

1 cup butter

1 teaspoon vanilla

2 cups flour

1 cup chopped pecans

3 heaping tablespoons powdered
sugar

Preheat oven to 300 degrees. In large bowl, cream butter. Add vanilla. Mix
well. Add flour. Mix well. Fold in pecans. Shape into crescents or fingers and
place on ungreased cookie sheet. Bake for 8 to 10 minutes or until golden
brown. Roll in powdered sugar while warm.

Yield: 15 servings

Angel Bites

1 cup finely chopped walnuts

½ cup unsweetened cocoa powder

1 cup sugar

3 tablespoons oil

8 egg whites

½ teaspoon salt

¼ cup powdered sugar

Preheat oven to 350 degrees. In large bowl, combine nuts, cocoa powder, sugar, and oil; set aside. In another bowl, beat egg whites and salt until stiff peaks form. Fold a third of beaten egg whites into nut mixture. Add remaining egg whites. Blend carefully. Spoon into greased or nonstick mini-muffin pans. Bake for 12 minutes. Cool for 5 minutes. Remove from pan and sprinkle with powdered sugar.

YIELD: 4 DOZEN

Coconut Pralines

2 cups chopped pecans

2½ cups grated coconut

1 teaspoon vanilla

2½ cups sugar

½ cup evaporated milk

½ cup corn syrup

½ cup butter

Measure out pecans, coconut, and vanilla. Set aside. In large, heavy saucepan, mix together sugar, milk, syrup, and butter. Bring to a rolling boil for 3 minutes. Remove from heat. Quickly add pecans, coconut, and vanilla. Stir for 4 minutes. Place by teaspoonful on waxed paper. Cool until hardened.

YIELD: 12 SERVINGS

Christmas Magic Bars

½ cup butter

1½ cups graham cracker crumbs

1 (6 ounce) package semisweet
    chocolate chips

1 cup flaked coconut

1 cup chopped pecans

1 (14 ounce) can sweetened
    condensed milk

Preheat oven to 350 degrees. Melt butter in 9x13-inch baking pan. Sprinkle graham cracker crumbs over butter. Layer as follows: chocolate morsels, coconut, pecans. Pour condensed milk over all. Do not stir. Bake for 25 minutes. Cool before cutting into squares.

YIELD: 2 DOZEN

Festive Cinnamon Delights

✻ · ✻ · ✻ · ✻ · ✻ · ✻

1 cup butter, softened

1 cup brown sugar

1 cup sugar

2 eggs, beaten

3½ cups flour

1 teaspoon baking soda

¼ teaspoon salt

1 tablespoon ground cinnamon

1 cup finely chopped pecans

Preheat oven to 350 degrees. In large bowl, cream butter and sugars. Add eggs. Beat on medium speed until fluffy. In separate bowl, combine flour, baking soda, salt, and cinnamon. Stir well. Add to creamed mixture. Beat well. Fold in pecans. Divide into 2 rolls. Wrap each roll in waxed paper and chill for 4 hours. Unwrap rolls and slice into ¼-inch slices. Place 2 inches apart on greased cookie sheets. Bake for 10 to 12 minutes. Cool.

YIELD: 6 DOZEN

Sugar and Spice Bars

❄ · ❄ · ❄ · ❄ · ❄

1 cup sugar

1 cup cooking oil

¼ cup honey

1 egg, beaten

2 cups flour

¼ teaspoon salt

1 teaspoon baking soda

1 teaspoon cinnamon

1 tablespoon mayonnaise

1 tablespoon water

1 cup powdered sugar

Preheat oven to 325 degrees. Combine sugar, oil, and honey. Mix well. Add egg, flour, salt, baking soda, and cinnamon. Mix well. Press into greased and floured 9x13-inch baking pan with sides. Bake for 15 minutes. Combine mayonnaise, water, and sugar. Mix well. Use to ice bars while warm. Cool before cutting into small bars.

YIELD: 4 DOZEN

Butter Yums

❄ · ❄ · ❄ · ❄ · ❄

2 cups salted butter, softened

2 cups powdered sugar

4 cups flour

1 teaspoon vanilla

Preheat oven to 350 degrees. In large bowl, cream butter and sugar. Add flour and vanilla. Roll into walnut-size balls. Place on ungreased cookie sheet, flattening with floured bottom of drinking glass. Bake for 15 minutes or until lightly brown. Cool on rack.

YIELD: 6 DOZEN

Christmas Almond Cookies

36 chocolate Kisses with almonds

1 cup butter, softened

½ cup sugar

1 teaspoon vanilla

1¾ cups flour

1¼ cups finely chopped, slivered almonds

½ teaspoon almond extract

1 cup powdered sugar, for rolling

Preheat oven to 375 degrees. Remove wrappers from chocolates; set aside. In large bowl, cream butter and sugar. Add vanilla and beat until fluffy. Add flour, almonds, and almond extract. Beat on low speed until well blended. For each cookie, take 1 tablespoon dough and shape it around a chocolate Kiss. Form balls. Each chocolate piece should be covered completely. Place on ungreased cookie sheet. Bake for 10 to 12 minutes or until cookies are set but not browned. Cool slightly. Remove from cookie sheet. While slightly warm, roll in powdered sugar. Cool completely. Store in tightly covered container. Roll again in powdered sugar just before serving.

YIELD: 3 DOZEN

Sunburst Bars

2 cups flour

½ cup powdered sugar

1 cup butter, softened

1 teaspoon lemon zest

4 eggs

2 cups sugar

¼ cup flour

1 teaspoon baking powder

¼ cup lemon juice

1 teaspoon lemon zest

1 cup powdered sugar

2½ tablespoons lemon juice

Preheat oven to 350 degrees. In large bowl with electric mixer, beat flour, sugar, butter, and lemon zest on low speed until crumbly. Press mixture evenly in bottom of ungreased 9x13-inch pan. Bake for 20 to 30 minutes or until light golden brown. In large bowl use a wire whisk to lightly beat eggs. Beat in sugar, flour, and baking powder. Add lemon juice and zest. Blend well. Pour filling evenly over warm base. Return to oven. Bake for 30 minutes. Cool for 1 hour. In small bowl, mix sugar and enough lemon juice for desired consistency until smooth. Spread over top and cut into bars. Store in refrigerator but bring to room temperature before serving.

Yield: 1 dozen

Merry Friendship Cookies

½ cup butter

½ cup vegetable oil

½ cup powdered sugar

1 egg, beaten

1 teaspoon lemon juice

1 teaspoon vanilla

1 teaspoon salt

1 teaspoon baking soda

2½ cups flour

Preheat oven to 350 degrees. In large bowl, cream butter, oil, and powdered sugar. Beat in egg, lemon juice, and vanilla. In another bowl, sift together salt, baking soda, and flour. Add to butter mixture. Mix well. Form into small balls. Place on greased cookie sheet. Flatten using sugar-coated bottom of drinking glass. Bake for 12 minutes.

YIELD: 2 DOZEN

Chocolate Snapper Cookies

1 (18.25 ounce) package chocolate cake mix

⅔ cup shortening

2 eggs, beaten

2½ cups pecans

1 (16 ounce) can chocolate frosting

Preheat oven to 350 degrees. In large bowl, beat together half the cake mix with shortening and eggs until smooth. Stir in remaining cake mix. For each cookie, place 3 pecan halves with ends touching on ungreased cookie sheet. Place 1 teaspoon dough in center of each group of pecans. Bake for 8 to 10 minutes or until centers are puffy and edges are set. Cool and remove from cookie sheet. Frost with chocolate frosting.

YIELD: 5 DOZEN

Butter Pecan Strips

24 graham crackers

1 cup butter

1 cup brown sugar

1 cup finely chopped pecans

Preheat oven to 400 degrees. Place whole graham crackers on ungreased cookie sheet with 1-inch sides. In saucepan, blend butter and brown sugar. Heat to boiling. Reduce heat and simmer for 2 minutes. Add chopped pecans. Spread mixture over crackers. Bake for 5 minutes. While warm, cut into strips where perforated on crackers. Place on rack to cool.

Yield: 2 dozen

Holiday Honey Drops

¾ cup butter, softened

¾ cup shortening

1½ cups firmly packed brown sugar

3 eggs

½ cup honey

1½ teaspoons vanilla

5 cups flour

4 teaspoons baking soda

1 (13 ounce) jar hazelnut spread

½ cup powdered sugar

In large bowl, cream butter and shortening. Blend in brown sugar. Add eggs one at a time, beating well after each. Stir in honey and vanilla. Stir in flour and baking soda. Cover and chill overnight. Preheat oven to 350 degrees. Shape dough into 1-inch balls. Place on ungreased baking sheet. Bake for 10 to 12 minutes or until firm. Cool. Sandwich 2 cookies together with hazelnut spread. Dust with powdered sugar. Store at room temperature.

Yield: 4 dozen

My Favorite Christmas Cookie Recipes

Recipe:

INGREDIENTS:

DIRECTIONS:

YIELD:

Recipe:

INGREDIENTS:

DIRECTIONS:

YIELD:

Recipe:

INGREDIENTS:

DIRECTIONS:

YIELD:

Recipe:

INGREDIENTS:

DIRECTIONS:

YIELD:

Recipe:

INGREDIENTS:

DIRECTIONS:

YIELD:

On the seventh day of Christmas my true love sent to me. . .

Seven Desserts a-Delighting

The spirit of Christmas fulfills
the greatest hunger of mankind.

LORING A. SCHULER

Lord Jesus, I hunger to know You better.
Show me new ways to put You at the center
of this wonderful Christmas season. Amen.

❋ · ❋ · ❋ · ❋ · ❋ · ❋

Glory to God in the highest,
and on earth peace, good will toward men.

LUKE 2:14

Christmas Angel Delight

1 store-bought angel food cake

1 pint whipping cream

1 pint sweetened frozen fruit, thawed

Break up angel food cake into large chunks. Whip cream and fold with fruit into cake pieces. Refrigerate in serving bowl for 2 to 3 hours.

YIELD: 10 TO 12 SERVINGS

Island Banana Dessert

6 bananas

1 tablespoon lemon juice

¼ teaspoon salt

3 tablespoons brown sugar

1 cup canned red cherries, drained (reserve syrup)

4 tablespoons butter

3 cups vanilla ice cream

Preheat oven to 400 degrees. Peel bananas and cut in half lengthwise. Arrange in greased, shallow baking dish. Sprinkle with lemon juice, salt, and sugar. Distribute cherries over banana mixture. Brush with reserved syrup. Top with butter and bake for 30 minutes or until bananas are soft. Generously baste with syrup twice more during baking process. Serve over ice cream.

YIELD: 6 SERVINGS

Raspberries in Vanilla Sauce

✺ · ✺ · ✺ · ✺ · ✺

1 quart raspberries, washed and drained

1 cup heavy cream

1 cup half-and-half

⅓ cup sugar

4 large egg yolks, beaten

½ teaspoon salt

1 teaspoon vanilla

Place berries in individual dessert bowls or small glasses. In heavy saucepan, gently whisk together cream, half-and-half, sugar, eggs, and salt. Cook over medium heat until thickened, but do not allow to boil. Remove from heat. Add vanilla. Mix well. Cool completely and refrigerate. When ready to serve, whisk gently. Pour over raspberries.

YIELD: 4 TO 6 SERVINGS

Mrs. Klaus's Orange Pie

✳ · ✳ · ✳ · ✳ · ✳ · ✳

2 cups vanilla wafer crumbs (about 60 cookies, crushed)

⅓ cup butter, melted

1 (8 ounce) package cream cheese, softened

1 (14 ounce) can sweetened condensed milk

1 (6 ounce) can orange juice concentrate, thawed

1 cup heavy cream, whipped

In small bowl, combine vanilla wafer crumbs and butter. Press firmly into bottom and sides of 9-inch pie plate. Chill. In large bowl, beat cream cheese until fluffy. Gradually beat in condensed milk and orange juice concentrate until smooth. Fold in whipped cream. Pour into crust. Chill for 2 hours or until set.

YIELD: 8 TO 10 SERVINGS

Elfin Magic Lemon Sherbet

2 (14½ ounce) cans evaporated milk

2 (6 ounce) cans frozen pink
   lemonade concentrate, undiluted

½ cup honey

Pour milk into a freezer container and place in freezer until half frozen. Transfer to bowl and beat with electric mixer until thick, fluffy, and about double in volume. Stir in lemonade concentrate and honey. Pour into freezer container and freeze until hard.

YIELD: 2 QUARTS

Eggnog Chiffon Pie

1½ cups sugar cookie crumbs

6 tablespoons butter

2 envelopes unflavored gelatin

⅓ cup water

2½ cups eggnog

1 cup heavy cream, whipped

1 teaspoon nutmeg

2 tablespoons cookie crumbs for
   garnish

8 maraschino cherries

In small bowl, mix 1½ cups cookie crumbs and butter until well blended. Press firmly and evenly into bottom and sides of ungreased 9-inch pie pan. Chill. In small saucepan, soften gelatin in water and stir over low heat until well dissolved. In bowl, mix gelatin and eggnog. Chill just until syrupy. Fold in whipped cream and spoon into crust. Sprinkle lightly with nutmeg. Chill until firm. Sprinkle additional cookie crumbs on top. Add cherries.

YIELD: 8 SERVINGS

Strawberries and Cream Loaf

❄ · ❄ · ❄ · ❄ · ❄ · ❄

1¾ cups flour

½ teaspoon baking powder

¼ teaspoon baking soda

½ teaspoon salt

¼ teaspoon cinnamon

½ cup butter, softened

¾ cup sugar

¼ cup light brown sugar

2 eggs, room temperature

½ cup sour cream, room temperature

1 teaspoon vanilla

1¼ cups fresh strawberries, coarsely chopped (not frozen)

¾ cup walnuts (optional)

Preheat oven to 350 degrees. In medium bowl, combine flour, baking powder, baking soda, salt, and cinnamon. Set aside. In large bowl, cream butter with electric mixer. Gradually add sugar and beat for 1 minute or until light and airy. Add brown sugar. Beat until creamy. Beat in eggs, one at a time. Beat in sour cream and vanilla. Add flour mixture and blend only until dry ingredients are moistened. Fold in strawberries and nuts. Pour into greased 8x4-inch loaf pan. Bake for 60 to 65 minutes. Let stand for 10 minutes in pan. Turn out on rack to cool.

YIELD: 8 TO 10 SERVINGS

Christmas in the South Buttermilk Pie

✳ · ✳ · ✳ · ✳ · ✳ · ✳

½ cup buttermilk

1¾ cups sugar

2 large eggs, beaten

3 tablespoons flour

⅛ teaspoon salt

1 stick butter, melted

1 teaspoon vanilla

1 teaspoon nutmeg

Preheat oven to 350 degrees. In large bowl, combine buttermilk and sugar. Add eggs and mix well. Add flour, salt, butter, and vanilla. Mix together until smooth. Pour into 9-inch pie shell. Sprinkle lightly with nutmeg. Bake for 45 minutes. Cool until filling is set.

YIELD: 8 TO 10 SERVINGS

Sensational Strawberry Sheet Cake

2 cups self-rising flour

2 cups sugar

4 eggs, beaten

1 cup vegetable oil

1 cup milk

¼ cup sweetened strawberries, mashed

1 (3 ounce) box strawberry gelatin

½ stick butter, softened

¾ cup powdered sugar

¼ cup sweetened strawberries, mashed

Preheat oven to 350 degrees. In large bowl, mix together flour, sugar, eggs, oil, milk, strawberries, and gelatin. Pour into greased 9×13-inch pan. Bake for 30 minutes. In small bowl, combine butter, sugar, and strawberries until smooth. Spread icing on cooled cake.

Yield: 12 to 15 servings

Cranberry Apple Pie

1½ cups sugar

¼ cup dry tapioca

1 cup whole cranberries

5 cups peeled, diced apples

2 (9 inch) piecrusts

1 tablespoon butter

Preheat oven to 400 degrees. Mix together sugar and tapioca. Add fruit. Let stand for 15 minutes. Pour into one of the piecrusts. Dot with butter. Cut remaining crust into ½-inch-wide strips. Weave strips in lattice design over fruit mixture. Seal edge and flute. Bake for 40 to 45 minutes.

Yield: 6 to 8 servings

Piña Colada Holiday Cake

1 cup unsalted butter, divided

3 (20 ounce) cans pineapple chunks, drained (juice reserved)

⅓ cup juice from pineapple chunks

1 (18.25 ounce) yellow cake mix

½ cup vegetable oil

2 eggs, beaten

3 tablespoons water

2 cups sweetened coconut flakes

Preheat oven to 350 degrees. In oven, melt ½ cup butter in 9x13-inch pan. Remove pan from oven; set aside. Combine pineapple chunks and juice. Pour into pan and spread. In large bowl, combine cake mix, oil, eggs, and water. Beat for 2 minutes. Spoon batter over pineapple chunks, covering completely. Sprinkle coconut on top. Cut remaining ½ cup butter into small cubes and sprinkle over coconut. Bake for 50 minutes, rotating every 15 minutes for even browning of coconut.

YIELD: 10 TO 12 SERVINGS

Cranberry Pudding

1 (3¾ ounce) package instant vanilla pudding mix

1¼ cups cold milk

½ cup sour cream

¼ teaspoon cinnamon

⅛ teaspoon nutmeg

½ cup jellied cranberry sauce

4 tablespoons flaked coconut

In large bowl, combine pudding mix, milk, sour cream, and spices. Beat until ingredients are well blended. Fold in cranberry sauce. Spoon into sherbet glasses. Chill. Sprinkle with coconut.

YIELD: 4 SERVINGS

Lime Bundt Cake

Cooking spray

Flour

1 (18.25 ounce) white or vanilla cake mix

1 cup lime yogurt (not fat free)

½ cup vegetable oil

4 eggs, beaten

1 tablespoon lime juice

1 tablespoon lime zest

2 cups powdered sugar

3 tablespoons butter, melted

3 tablespoons lime juice

2 tablespoons milk

⅛ teaspoon salt

Lime zest, for garnish

Preheat oven to 350 degrees. Coat 12-cup Bundt pan or 10-inch fluted tube pan with cooking spray. Dust with flour. In large bowl, use electric mixer on low to mix together cake mix, yogurt, oil, eggs, lime juice, and lime zest until moistened. Beat on medium speed for 2 minutes. Spread evenly in prepared pan. Bake for 40 to 44 minutes. Cool in pan for 15 minutes. Remove to wire rack. Cool completely. In large bowl, mix powdered sugar, butter, lime juice, milk, and salt with whisk. Once combined, spoon over cake. Garnish with lime zest.

Yield: 12 servings

Double Chocolate Cola Cake

2 cups sugar

2 cups flour

½ teaspoon salt

1 cup cola

½ cup vegetable oil

½ cup butter

3 tablespoons unsweetened cocoa

2 eggs

½ cup buttermilk

1 teaspoon baking soda

1 teaspoon vanilla

½ cup butter

3 tablespoons unsweetened cocoa

6 tablespoons cream or milk

1 teaspoon vanilla

3¾ cups powdered sugar

Preheat oven to 350 degrees. In large bowl, combine sugar, flour, and salt; set aside. In saucepan, mix together cola, oil, butter, and cocoa. Bring to boil. Pour boiling cola mixture over flour mixture and beat well. Add eggs, buttermilk, baking soda, and vanilla. Beat well. Pour mixture into a greased and floured 9x13-inch baking pan and bake for 20 to 25 minutes. Remove from pan. Cool for 10 minutes. In saucepan, combine butter, cocoa, and cream or milk. Heat until butter melts. Beat in vanilla. Beat in powdered sugar. Spread warm icing on cake.

Yield: 12 servings

Heavenly Fruit Pie

✳ · ✳ · ✳ · ✳ · ✳

1 (12 ounce) can sweetened condensed milk

¼ cup lemon juice

1 cup flaked coconut

1 cup frozen strawberries, thawed

1 (8 ounce) can crushed pineapple

1 cup pecans

1 (9 ounce) tub whipped topping

1 (9 inch) graham cracker piecrust

In large bowl, combine condensed milk and lemon juice. Blend well. Add coconut, strawberries, pineapple, pecans, and whipped topping. Blend carefully. Pour into graham cracker crust. Chill for at least 1 hour before serving.

Yield: 8 servings

Easy Gingerbread

✳ · ✳ · ✳ · ✳ · ✳

½ cup boiling water

½ cup shortening

½ cup brown sugar

½ cup molasses

1 egg, beaten

½ teaspoon salt

½ teaspoon baking powder

½ teaspoon baking soda

¾ teaspoon ginger

¾ teaspoon cinnamon

¼ teaspoon cloves

1½ cups flour

Preheat oven to 350 degrees. In large bowl, pour boiling water over shortening and stir. Add brown sugar, molasses, and egg. Stir. In separate bowl, sift together salt, baking powder, baking soda, spices, and flour. Add to mixture. Beat with mixer until smooth. Pour into 8x8-inch pan. Bake for 35 minutes.

Yield: 12 servings

Cream Cheese Peach Pie

Cooking spray

1 (18.25 ounce) package white or yellow cake mix

⅓ cup butter, room temperature

2 large eggs, divided

1 (29 ounce) can peach slices, drained

8 ounces cream cheese, room temperature

⅓ cup sugar

1 teaspoon vanilla

Preheat oven to 350 degrees. Spray 9x13-inch pan with cooking spray. In large bowl, combine cake mix, butter, and 1 egg. Mix until crumbly. Set aside 1½ cups crumbs for topping. Press remaining crumbs in bottom of prepared pan. Bake for 10 minutes. Spoon peaches into partially baked crust. In large bowl, combine cream cheese, sugar, remaining egg, and vanilla. Beat with mixer until creamy. Spoon over peaches. Sprinkle with reserved crumbs. Bake for 30 minutes. Chill for 30 minutes before serving.

Yield: 8 to 10 servings

Choco-Christmas Cobbler

¾ cup sugar

1 cup self-rising flour

2 tablespoons unsweetened cocoa

½ cup milk

3 tablespoons butter, melted

1 teaspoon vanilla

½ cup sugar

½ cup brown sugar

¼ cup unsweetened cocoa

1½ cups hot water

Preheat oven to 350 degrees. Mix together sugar, flour, cocoa, milk, butter, and vanilla. Spread into greased 11×7-inch glass baking dish. In another bowl, mix together remaining sugars and cocoa. Sprinkle evenly over the first mixture. Pour 1½ cups hot water gently over all. Do not mix. Bake for 40 minutes.

YIELD: 8 TO 10 SERVINGS

No-Bake Fruit Cake

½ cup butter

1 (10 ounce) package marshmallows

1 (10 ounce) jar red cherries and juice

1 (15 ounce) box raisins

1 cup pecans

16 ounces candied fruit

1 (13.5 ounce) box crushed graham crackers

In microwave, melt butter and marshmallows together. Transfer to large bowl. Add cherries with juice, raisins, nuts, candied fruit, and graham crackers. Mix well. Pack into 2 waxed paper–lined, 9x5-inch loaf pans. Wet hands and press firm. Refrigerate for one day before slicing.

YIELD: 2 LOAVES

Chocolate Caramel Pecan Cake

✳ · ✳ · ✳ · ✳ · ✳

2 to 3 tablespoons butter, melted

1 cup superfine sugar, divided, plus 1 tablespoon

16 ounces bittersweet or semisweet chocolate, finely chopped

1 cup unsalted butter

8 large eggs, separated, at room temperature

¼ teaspoon salt

2 tablespoons water

1 teaspoon vanilla

½ teaspoon cream of tartar

1 cup sugar

5 tablespoons water

⅛ teaspoon cream of tartar

1 cup pecan halves

¾ cup heavy cream

¼ teaspoon salt

Preheat oven to 350 degrees. Brush 10-inch springform pan with 2 to 3 tablespoons butter and coat with 1 tablespoon sugar. Tap out excess. Melt chocolate and 1 cup butter in microwave. Stir until smooth. Transfer to large mixing bowl. Set aside. Beat egg yolks and salt on medium speed until smooth. Gradually add ½ cup sugar and beat until thick. Whisk in water and vanilla. Gradually whisk egg mixture into melted chocolate. Beat egg whites and cream of tartar with mixer on low until frothy. Add remaining ½ cup sugar and beat on high to form soft peaks. Stir a third of egg whites into chocolate. Fold in remaining egg whites. Pour into pan. Bake for 25 minutes. In large saucepan, combine sugar, water, and cream of tartar. Cook until sugar dissolves, stirring often. Bring to boil. When mixture turns deep amber color, remove from heat and stir in pecans, cream, and salt. Turn to low heat and stir until caramel thickens. Spoon over cake while warm.

YIELD: 10 SERVINGS

My Favorite Christmas Dessert Recipes

Recipe:

INGREDIENTS:

DIRECTIONS:

YIELD:

Recipe:

INGREDIENTS:

DIRECTIONS:

YIELD:

Recipe:

INGREDIENTS:

DIRECTIONS:

YIELD:

Recipe:

INGREDIENTS:

DIRECTIONS:

YIELD:

Recipe:

INGREDIENTS:

DIRECTIONS:

YIELD:

On the eighth day of Christmas my true love sent to me. . .

Eight Kids a-Cooking

It is good to be children sometimes,
and never better than at Christmas,
when its mighty Founder
was a child Himself.

CHARLES DICKENS

Heavenly Father, thank You for all the blessings
of the Christmas season. Thank You for
our children, and thank You for the privilege
of being called Your children. Amen.

Thanks be unto God for his unspeakable gift.

2 CORINTHIANS 9:15

Breakfast Fruit Toast

2 slices bread, lightly toasted

1 cup ricotta cheese

1 cup sliced fresh or frozen strawberries

2 teaspoons sugar

Spread ricotta cheese over toasted bread. Top with strawberries and sprinkle with sugar. Broil lightly for 1 minute.

YIELD: 2 SERVINGS

Frog-Eye Fruit Salad

1 pound acini de pepe pasta

1 (20 ounce) can crushed pineapple

1 (16 ounce) can mandarin oranges

1 cup sugar

½ teaspoon salt

2 tablespoons flour

3 egg yolks, beaten

4 cups mini marshmallows

1 (8 ounce) tub whipped topping

Cook pasta in boiling water until tender. Drain, transfer pasta to bowl, and set aside. Drain juice from pineapple and oranges and set aside; do not discard juice. Place fruit in refrigerator. In small saucepan, combine juice, sugar, salt, and flour. Blend well. Cook until thickened, stirring constantly. Remove from heat. Wait for 5 minutes and stir in egg yolks. Stir well. Return to burner and cook another minute. Pour over cooled pasta. Cover and refrigerate overnight. Add fruit, marshmallows, and whipped topping. Chill until served.

YIELD: 6 CUPS

Tiny's Breakfast Casserole

* · * · * · * · * · *

2 tablespoons butter

8 slices bread, cubed

1 pound ground sausage, uncooked

7 eggs, beaten

½ cup milk

2½ teaspoons dry mustard

1 (22.6 ounce) can cream of mushroom soup

½ cup milk

½ cup grated cheddar cheese

With 2 tablespoons butter, grease bottom and sides of a 9x11-inch baking pan. Spread bread cubes on bottom of pan. With fingers, break up sausage and distribute over bread cubes. In medium bowl, mix together eggs, milk, and mustard. Pour evenly over bread and sausage. Place in refrigerator overnight. In the morning, preheat oven to 300 degrees. Combine soup and milk. Pour over casserole. Sprinkle with cheese. Bake for 1 hour.

YIELD: 6 TO 8 SERVINGS

Rudolph's Cheesy Potato Soup

* · ❄ · ❋ · ❋ · ❄ · ❋ · ❋ *

1 medium to large baking potato

2 (10 ounce) cans cheddar cheese soup

1½ cups canned chicken broth

¼ cup bacon, cooked and crumbled

½ cup sour cream

⅓ cup chopped green onion

Cook potato in microwave for 8 minutes on high. When potato is cool enough to handle, cut into small pieces (about ½ inch each); set aside. In medium saucepan, combine cheddar soup, chicken broth, and bacon. Bring to simmer over medium heat, stirring occasionally. Stir in the potato and cook 5 minutes longer. Spoon into bowls and top with sour cream and chopped green onion.

YIELD: 6 SERVINGS

Santa's Strawberry Fudge

✳ · ✳ · ✳ · ✳ · ✳

1 (12 ounce) bag white candy melts or white chocolate chips

1 (16 ounce) tub strawberry frosting

Line 9x9–inch square pan with parchment paper. In small microwave-safe bowl, microwave candy melts or chocolate on medium for 30-second intervals, stirring between intervals until smooth. Add frosting. Stir until mixed well. Pour mixture into prepared pan. Refrigerate until completely set. Cut into pieces.

YIELD: 20 PIECES

Holiday Trail Mix

✳ · ✳ · ✳ · ✳ · ✳

⅔ cup honey-nut flavored cereal

⅔ cup small chocolate-covered candies

⅔ cup mini pretzels

⅔ cup raisins

In medium bowl, gently mix together cereal, candies, pretzels, and raisins. Store in sealed plastic bags until ready to serve.

YIELD: 4 SERVINGS

Rock Candy

2 cups sugar

½ cup corn syrup

½ cup water

½ teaspoon flavored oil (lemon, cinnamon, peppermint, etc.)

1 squirt food coloring, any color

1 cup powdered sugar

In heavy saucepan, boil sugar, corn syrup, and water until mixture reaches 300 degrees or hard crack stage. Remove from heat. Add oil and food coloring. Pour quickly onto greased cookie sheet. When mixture cools, there will be one hard slab of candy. Press a hard object into center of candy to fracture it into manageable pieces. Place a few shards at a time in bag of powdered sugar and shake. Transfer to colander and shake to remove all but light sugar dusting.

YIELD: 1½ POUNDS

Mini Banana Cream Cookie Pies

✳ · ✳ · ✳ · ✳ · ✳

1 (16.5 ounce) tube sugar cookie dough

2 cups milk

1 (3¾ ounce) box instant banana cream pudding mix

2 bananas

1½ cups whipped topping

Preheat oven to 350 degrees. Grease 24-cup mini-muffin pan. Divide sugar cookie dough into 24 pieces and form into balls. Place dough in prepared muffin cups. Bake dough for 15 to 18 minutes until golden brown. Remove from oven and use bottom of small shot glass to make depression in each cup. While cups are cooling, combine milk and pudding mix in small saucepan. Over medium heat, stir frequently until pudding thickens. Place pudding in refrigerator to chill. Transfer cookie cups to cooling rack. When pudding is chilled, slice bananas into 24 slices and place 1 slice on the bottom of each cookie cup. Spoon pudding over each banana slice. Add spoon of whipped cream.

Yield: 24 servings

Crunch Sticks

1 (10 count) tube refrigerated biscuits

¾ cup crispy rice cereal, crushed

1 tablespoon caraway or celery seeds

1 teaspoon salt

¼ cup milk

Preheat oven to 450 degrees. Cut biscuits in half. Roll each piece to pencil thickness and about 4 inches long. Combine cereal, seeds, and salt in shallow pan. Roll sticks in milk first and then cereal mixture. Place on greased baking sheet. Bake for 10 minutes.

YIELD: 20 STICKS

Prancer's Lemon Drops

1 (18.25 ounce) lemon cake mix

2 eggs, beaten

½ cup oil

3 tablespoons water

⅛ teaspoon lemon juice

Preheat oven 350 degrees. Mix together cake mix, eggs, oil, water, and lemon juice. Drop by teaspoonfuls onto greased cookie sheet. Bake for 8 minutes.

YIELD: 12 TO 18 SERVINGS.

Fried Cinnamon Bananas

* · * · * · * · * · *

2 slightly overripe bananas

2 tablespoons sugar

1 teaspoon cinnamon

¼ teaspoon nutmeg

Olive oil spray

Slice bananas into ⅓-inch rounds; set aside. In small bowl, combine sugar, cinnamon, and nutmeg. Set aside. Spray large skillet with olive oil. On medium heat, cook banana rounds for 3 minutes. Sprinkle half the cinnamon mixture over bananas. Flip bananas and sprinkle with remaining cinnamon mixture. Cook for 2 minutes or until bananas are soft and warm.

YIELD: 2 SERVINGS

Caramel Doodles

2 (8 count) tubes refrigerated
   crescent rolls

16 caramels

2 cups sugar

1 tablespoon cinnamon

Preheat oven to 350 degrees. Wrap one caramel in each crescent roll and form balls; set aside. Combine sugar and cinnamon. Roll balls in cinnamon/sugar mixture. Place on baking sheet 1 inch apart. Bake for 12 minutes or until slightly puffy. Serve warm.

YIELD: 16 SERVINGS

Banana Fritters

✳ · ✳ · ✳ · ✳ · ✳

2 cups cornflakes

1 tablespoon sugar

5 ripe bananas, peeled

¼ cup orange juice

1 tablespoon butter

Preheat oven to 400 degrees. Place cornflakes and sugar in sealable plastic bag, seal it, and use your fist to crush cornflakes into crumbs. Pour into long bowl or pan; set aside. Cut bananas in half lengthwise and dip in orange juice. Roll bananas in crumbs. Place on lightly greased cookie sheet. Dot with butter. Bake for 15 minutes.

YIELD: 4 TO 6 SERVINGS

North Pole Cracker Pizzas

✳ · ✳ · ✳ · ✳ · ✳

24 round snack crackers

1 cup strawberry cream cheese

4 strawberries, sliced

Spread crackers with cream cheese. Add sliced strawberries.

YIELD: 24 MINI PIZZAS

Tasty Cornbread

2 cups yellow cornmeal

1 cup self-rising flour

1 egg, beaten

½ cup sour cream

1½ cups milk

Preheat oven to 400 degrees. Grease medium cast-iron skillet and warm it in the oven. Mix together cornmeal, flour, egg, sour cream, and milk. Pour mixture into skillet. Bake for 25 minutes or until golden brown.

Yield: 8 servings

Holiday Coconut Cake

1 (18.25 ounce) white cake mix

½ cup oil

2 eggs, beaten

3 tablespoons water

1 cup sour cream

1 cup sugar

16 ounces whipped topping

1 (12 ounce) package flaked coconut

Preheat oven to 350 degrees. Combine cake mix with oil, eggs, and water. Pour into three 8-inch cake pans. Bake for 20 minutes. Cool completely. Mix sour cream and sugar together. Place whipped topping in large bowl and fold sour cream mixture into it. Spread in between layers and over cake. Sprinkle top of cake with coconut. Refrigerate.

YIELD: 8 TO 10 SERVINGS

Blitzen's Bread Pudding

✻ · ✻ · ✻ · ✻ · ✻

2 cups sugar	2 cups milk
4 eggs, beaten	¼ cup butter
1½ teaspoons vanilla	1 tablespoon maple syrup
½ teaspoon nutmeg	6 biscuits

Preheat oven to 400 degrees. Mix together sugar, eggs, vanilla, nutmeg, milk, butter, and maple syrup. Pour into 2-quart baking dish. Break each biscuit into 4 pieces. Drop into liquid mixture. Bake for 1 hour or until brown on top.

YIELD: 8 SERVINGS

Cola Fruit Salad

✻ · ✻ · ✻ · ✻ · ✻

1 envelope unflavored gelatin	1½ cups cola or ginger ale
2 tablespoons sugar	1½ cups fruit cocktail, drained
¼ cup water	½ cup nuts, any kind
Juice from 1 lemon	1 small tub whipped topping

In saucepan, mix together gelatin and sugar. Add water and lemon juice. Place over low heat. Keep stirring until gelatin and sugar are dissolved. Remove from heat. Add cola or ginger ale. Stir and chill until thickened but not completely set. Add fruit. Return to refrigerator and chill until set. Top with nuts and whipped topping.

YIELD: 6 SERVINGS

Grilled Peanut Butter Sandwiches

8 bread slices

8 tablespoons peanut butter

8 teaspoons jam or jelly

8 tablespoons mayonnaise or softened butter

Spread peanut butter evenly on one side of 4 slices of bread. Spread jam or jelly evenly on one side of other 4 slices of bread. Close to make 4 sandwiches. Spread mayonnaise or butter on outside of sandwiches. Place on griddle. Grill both sides until brown.

YIELD: 4 SANDWICHES

Hot Holiday Hamwiches

¼ cup butter, softened

2 tablespoons mustard

2 tablespoons chopped onion

8 slices wheat or rye bread

4 slices baked ham

4 slices swiss cheese

8 tablespoons softened butter, for grilling

Combine butter, mustard, and onion. Spread on one side of 4 slices of bread. Top each with 1 slice ham, 1 slice cheese, and remaining slice of bread. Butter outside of hamwiches. Place on griddle. Grill until brown. Flip and grill other side.

YIELD: 4 HAMWICHES

My Favorite Christmas Kids' Recipes

Recipe:

INGREDIENTS:

DIRECTIONS:

YIELD:

Recipe:

INGREDIENTS:

DIRECTIONS:

YIELD:

Recipe: ....

INGREDIENTS: ....

....

....

DIRECTIONS: ....

....

....

....

....

YIELD: ....

Recipe: ....

INGREDIENTS: ....

....

....

DIRECTIONS: ....

....

....

....

....

YIELD: ....

Recipe: ....

INGREDIENTS: ....

....

....

DIRECTIONS: ....

....

....

....

....

YIELD: ....

On the ninth day of Christmas my true love sent to me. . .

Which Christmas is the most vivid to me?
It's always the next one.

Joanne Woodward

Lord God, thank You for Your presence with us as we sit down together around the Christmas table in honor of Your birthday. Amen.

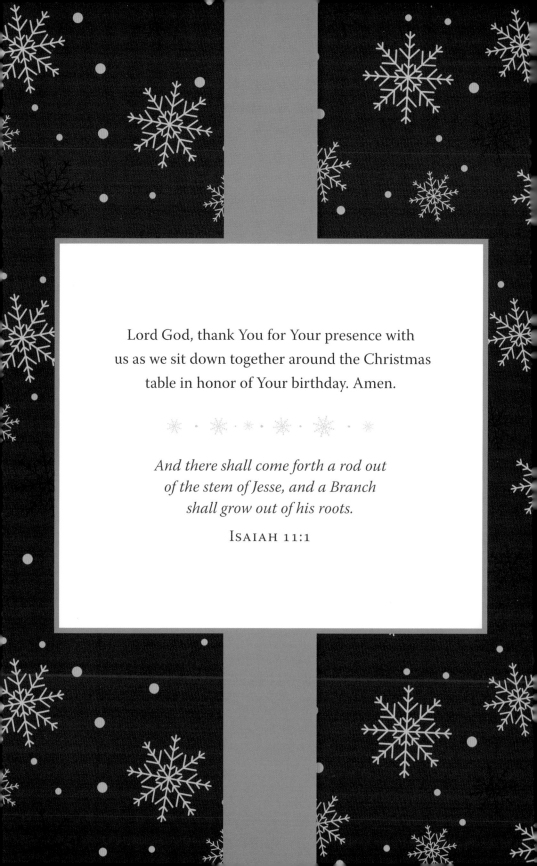

And there shall come forth a rod out of the stem of Jesse, and a Branch shall grow out of his roots.

ISAIAH 11:1

Turkey Pot Pie

⁂ · ⁂ · ⁂ · ⁂ · ⁂

⅓ cup butter, melted

1 cup diced potatoes

1 cup diced onion

1 cup diced celery

1 cup diced carrots

½ cup flour

2 cups chicken broth

1 cup half-and-half

1 teaspoon salt

¼ teaspoon pepper

4 cups turkey, cooked and chopped

2 (9 inch) piecrusts

Preheat oven to 400 degrees. In saucepan, melt butter and sauté potatoes, onion, celery, and carrots for 10 minutes. Add flour to mixture, stirring well. Cook for 1 minute, stirring constantly; set aside. In bowl, combine broth and half-and-half. Gradually stir into vegetable mixture. Cook over medium heat, stirring constantly, until thickened and bubbly. Add salt and pepper. Blend well. Add turkey and stir well. Place 1 piecrust in bottom of shallow 2-quart casserole dish. Pour in turkey mixture. Top with second piecrust. Crimp edges. Bake for 40 minutes or until top is browned and bubbling.

YIELD: 12 TO 15 SERVINGS

Chicken Noodle Casserole

5 ounces dry egg noodles

2 tablespoons unsalted butter

½ small onion, chopped

2 tablespoons flour

1½ cups milk

1½ cups shredded cheddar cheese

2 cups chopped rotisserie chicken meat, skin and bones discarded

1½ cups frozen peas

1 teaspoon salt

1 teaspoon pepper

¼ cup panko bread crumbs

¼ cup shredded Parmesan cheese

Preheat oven to 400 degrees. Grease 2-quart casserole dish. Cook noodles in boiling, salted water until tender. Drain and set aside. In large saucepan, melt butter over medium heat. Add onion and sauté for 4 minutes. Sprinkle flour over onion and stir until well blended. Cook for 1 minute. Add milk and bring to simmer. When mixture thickens, turn off heat and add cheese. Stir until melted. Add chicken, peas, and noodles. Stir. Add salt and pepper. Pour mixture into prepared 2-quart casserole dish. Sprinkle with bread crumbs and Parmesan. Bake for 12 minutes or until browned and cheese is melted. Serve hot.

Yield: 8 servings

Turkey Tetrazzini

❄ · ❄ · ❄ · ❄ · ❄

1 cup shredded Parmesan cheese, divided

1 (10.75 ounce) can cream of mushroom soup (undiluted)

1 (10 ounce) container refrigerated Alfredo sauce

1 (3½ ounce) can sliced mushrooms, drained

½ cup slivered almonds, toasted

½ cup chicken broth

¼ cup dry cooking sherry

½ teaspoon salt

¼ teaspoon pepper

3 cups chopped, cooked turkey

7 ounces cooked vermicelli

Preheat oven to 350 degrees. Set aside ½ cup Parmesan cheese. In large bowl, combine remaining Parmesan with mushroom soup, Alfredo sauce, mushrooms, almonds, chicken broth, sherry, salt, and pepper. Stir in turkey and pasta. Pour into lightly greased 8x11-inch casserole dish. Sprinkle with reserved shredded Parmesan and bake for 30 minutes.

YIELD: 8 SERVINGS

· ·

Aunt Jule's Baked Chicken

❄ · ❄ · ❄ · ❄ · ❄

6 small or 4 medium chicken breasts

½ cup Parmesan cheese

1 cup plain Greek yogurt

1 teaspoon garlic powder

1½ teaspoons seasoned salt

½ teaspoon pepper

Preheat oven to 375 degrees. Place chicken breasts in 9x11-inch greased casserole dish. Combine cheese, yogurt, garlic powder, salt, and pepper. Spread evenly over chicken. Bake, uncovered, for 45 minutes.

YIELD: 4 TO 6 SERVINGS

Orange Chicken

1 tablespoon butter

½ cup slivered almonds

3 cups diced cooked chicken

2 tablespoons cornstarch

1 cup chicken broth

1 (6 ounce) can orange juice concentrate, thawed and undiluted

1 teaspoon molasses

1 teaspoon soy sauce

½ teaspoon salt

1 (6 ounce) package wild rice

In saucepan, melt butter and sauté almonds until brown. Add chicken. Set aside. In bowl, mix together cornstarch, chicken broth, orange juice concentrate, molasses, soy sauce, and salt until well blended. Add to saucepan and stir over low heat until thickened. In separate pot, cook rice until tender. When serving, spoon chicken mixture over rice.

Yield: 4 servings

Easy Cheesy Holiday Beef

5 to 6 medium potatoes, diced and cooked

2 pounds round or skirt steak, diced and cooked

¼ cup butter

2 large onions, sliced

1 (16 ounce) can tomatoes, undrained

8 ounces mozzarella cheese, shredded

½ cup grated Parmesan cheese

Preheat oven to 350 degrees. Mix potatoes and beef and place in greased 2-quart casserole pan. In small skillet, melt butter and sauté onions for 5 minutes. Add onions and tomatoes to casserole and stir lightly. Top with cheeses. Bake for 25 minutes or until lightly browned.

Yield: 6 servings

Golden Glazed Ham

❄ · ❄ · ❄ · ❄ · ❄ · ❄

1 (5 to 6 pound) cooked ham

24 whole cloves

2 teaspoons orange zest

1 cup orange juice

½ cup brown sugar, firmly packed

4 teaspoons cornstarch

1½ teaspoons dry mustard

Preheat oven to 350 degrees. Score ham with diagonal cuts in a diamond pattern. Push clove ends into scored intersections in ham. Place in shallow roasting pan. Bake for 1½ hours for rump or 2 hours for shank. In saucepan, combine orange zest, juice, sugar, cornstarch and mustard. Cook and stir over medium heat until thickened and bubbly. Cook and stir for 2 minutes longer. When ham is finished roasting, remove from oven and brush with glaze. Return to oven and bake for an additional 25 minutes. Let stand for 15 minutes before carving.

YIELD: 16 TO 20 SERVINGS

Holiday Slow-Cooker Pulled Pork

1 medium onion, cut into 8 pieces

2½ to 3 pound pork butt

2 garlic cloves, minced

1½ teaspoons dry mustard

¼ teaspoon cayenne pepper

¼ teaspoon salt

⅛ teaspoon black pepper

¼ cup apple cider vinegar

3 tablespoons Worcestershire sauce

2 (12 ounce) cans cola

1 (10 ounce) jar barbecue sauce

1 (8 count) package hamburger buns

Place onion pieces in bottom of slow-cooker. Layer pork on top. In small bowl, combine garlic, mustard, cayenne pepper, salt, black pepper, cider vinegar, and Worcestershire sauce. Pour over pork. Pour cola on top and cook on high for 4½ hours or low for 8 hours. Remove meat from slow-cooker to cool. Shred with forks. Place shredded pork back into the slow-cooker and cook on low for 1 hour. Drain off juices. Add barbecue sauce and toss until well mixed. Serve on hamburger buns.

YIELD: 6 TO 8 SERVINGS

Granny's Baked Penne

½ pound ground beef

½ pound Italian sausage

1 teaspoon Italian seasoning

1 (12 ounce) jar spaghetti sauce

8 ounces of penne pasta, uncooked

½ cup water

4 ounces shredded cheddar or Colby cheese

Preheat oven to 350 degrees. In skillet, brown ground beef and sausage. Add seasoning. Stir well. Add spaghetti sauce. Stir. Place uncooked pasta in greased 9x13-inch baking pan. Pour meat sauce over the top and spread to cover. Add water evenly over all. Bake for 45 minutes. Sprinkle top with cheese and bake for another 15 minutes or until cheese is bubbly.

Yield: 6 servings

Shrimp Fried Rice

3 tablespoons sesame oil

1 cup frozen peas and carrots (thawed)

1 small onion, chopped

¼ cup green onion, chopped

1 teaspoon minced garlic

2 eggs, slightly beaten

3 cups cooked white rice

¼ cup soy sauce

In large skillet or wok, heat oil on medium-high heat. Add peas and carrots, onion, green onion, and garlic. Stir-fry until tender. Lower heat to medium low. Push mixture off to one side. Pour eggs onto the empty side of skillet or wok and stir-fry until scrambled. Add rice and soy sauce. Blend all ingredients together well. Stir-fry until thoroughly heated.

Yield: 4 to 6 servings

Festive Chicken Lasagna

* · * · * · * · * · *

9 lasagna noodles

4 medium chicken breasts, cooked and cut into chunks

¼ cup diced onion

½ cup mushrooms, sliced

1 (10.75 ounce) can cream of chicken soup

1 (10.75 ounce) can cream of mushroom soup

1 cup sour cream

¼ teaspoon salt

⅛ teaspoon pepper

3 cups grated cheddar cheese

1 cup grated Parmesan cheese

Preheat oven to 350 degrees. Grease 9x13-inch baking pan. Cook noodles in salted, boiling water until slightly tender. Drain and set aside. In large bowl, blend together chicken, onion, mushrooms, soups, and sour cream. In prepared pan, place 3 noodles side by side. Season with salt and pepper. Over noodles layer a third of chicken mixture and then a third of cheeses. Repeat this layering three times. Bake for 40 minutes or until lightly browned. Cool for 5 minutes before cutting.

YIELD: 6 SERVINGS

Grecian Lasagna

¾ pound ground beef

¼ cup chopped onion

1 garlic clove, minced

1 (32 ounce) jar spaghetti sauce

6 lasagna noodles

2 (4 ounce) packages feta cheese, crumbled

1 (8 ounce) package Monterey Jack cheese, shredded

Preheat oven to 350 degrees. In large skillet, brown meat. Drain. Add onion and garlic. Cook until tender. Stir in spaghetti sauce and simmer for 20 minutes. Boil noodles in salted water until tender. Drain. Set aside. In small bowl, combine cheeses. Spread ½ cup sauce in bottom of 12x8-inch baking dish. Lay three noodles over sauce. Spoon and spread enough sauce to cover noodles. Sprinkle with cheese. Place the remaining noodles on top of cheese. Add remaining meat sauce. Sprinkle with remaining cheese. Bake for 30 minutes. Let stand for 10 minutes before cutting.

Yield: 8 servings

Beef Tips and Noodles

✳ · ✳ · ✳ · ✳ · ✳

1 cup sliced mushrooms

2 (12 ounce) jars brown gravy

1 (10.75 ounce) can cream of mushroom soup

1 (1.9 ounce) package of onion soup mix

1½ pounds of thin-cut round steak, uncooked and cubed

⅔ cup water

½ teaspoon salt

½ teaspoon pepper

1 (12 ounce) package egg noodles

In Crock-Pot or slow-cooker, combine mushrooms, gravy, soup, soup mix, steak, water, salt, and pepper. Blend well. Cook on low for 6 to 8 hours or high for 4 to 6 hours. When ready to serve, boil egg noodles in salted water until tender. Place serving of noodles on each plate and cover with beef tips.

Yield: 6 servings

Yummy Chicken in a Pot

½ cup butter

4 to 5 medium chicken breasts

1 teaspoon salt

1 teaspoon pepper

1 teaspoon garlic powder

4 to 5 potatoes, peeled and quartered

6 to 8 carrots, cubed

1 onion, sliced

1 teaspoon salt, to be added later

In large Dutch oven or broiler pan, melt butter on stovetop. Season chicken breasts with salt, pepper, and garlic powder. Place in pan. With heat on high, brown on both sides. Turn heat to low and layer potatoes, carrots, and onion on top. Sprinkle with additional salt. Cover and cook for 1 hour.

YIELD: 6 SERVINGS

Santa's Favorite Chicken Casserole

2 cups cooked chicken, cubed

1½ cups cooked rice

1 cup mayonnaise

1 (10.75 ounce) can cream of mushroom soup

1 (10 ounce) box frozen broccoli

1 (5 ounce) can water chestnuts, drained

¼ cup butter

8 ounces of butter crackers (2 sleeves)

Preheat oven to 350 degrees. In large bowl, blend together chicken, rice, mayonnaise, soup, broccoli, and water chestnuts. Place in 2-quart greased casserole dish. In small bowl, melt butter in microwave. Crumble crackers into butter. Blend until moistened. Sprinkle over casserole. Bake for 25 minutes.

YIELD: 4 TO 6 SERVINGS

Silver Bell Beefwiches

* · ❄ · * · ❄ · * · ❄ · · ❄

1 cup green pepper strips

1 medium onion, sliced

1 tablespoon butter

1 pound roast beef, thinly sliced

1 (8 ounce) jar processed cheese spread

6 (6 inch) french bread rolls, partially split

In large saucepan, sauté pepper strips and onion in butter. Remove from heat. Add meat. Stir gently until heated throughout. Warm cheese spread in microwave. Fill rolls with steak mixture. Pour cheese sauce over steak mixture. Serve hot.

Yield: 6 beefwiches

Holiday Skillet Chicken

* · ❄ · * · ❄ · * · · ❄

3 tablespoons oil

2½ pounds chicken legs

1 pound sweet potatoes, peeled and thinly sliced

1 cup unsweetened pineapple juice

⅓ cup minced celery leaves

1 bay leaf, crumbled

1 large green or red pepper, sliced

1 medium onion, sliced

2 cups frozen peas, thawed

In large skillet, heat oil and brown chicken legs on all sides. Spoon off fat. Add sweet potatoes, pineapple juice, celery leaves, and bay leaf. Simmer, covered, for 20 minutes or until chicken is done and sweet potatoes are tender. Add pepper slices, onion, and peas. Cook until tender and crisp.

Yield: 4 servings

Christmas Eve Stir Fry

1½ pounds boneless pork, cut into strips

1 (8 ounce) bottle French dressing

1 cup water

1 teaspoon ginger

¼ teaspoon ground red pepper

2 tablespoons soy sauce

1 tablespoon cornstarch

2 cups shredded bok choy or lettuce

½ cup red pepper strips

½ cup celery slices, diagonally cut

4 green onions, cut into 1-inch pieces

3 cups cooked instant rice

In large skillet, brown meat in ¼ cup dressing over low heat. Add remaining dressing, water, and seasonings. Cover and simmer for 30 minutes. In small bowl, combine soy sauce and cornstarch. Stir into mixture. Stirring constantly, cook until mixture boils and thickens. Stir in vegetables. Cook until heated throughout. Serve over rice.

YIELD: 6 SERVINGS

Day-after-Christmas Slow-Cooker Spaghetti

❄ · ❄ · ❄ · ❄ · ❄ · ❄

1½ pounds ground beef or turkey

1 small onion, chopped

2 (14.5 ounce) cans diced tomatoes, undrained

2 (15 ounce) cans tomato sauce

1 (6 ounce) can tomato paste

2 teaspoons dried Italian seasoning

1 (16 ounce) package spaghetti

Place ground beef or turkey, onion, tomatoes, tomato sauce, tomato paste, and Italian seasoning into slow-cooker. Mix well, breaking up meat. Cook on low for 7 hours or high for 4 hours. Shortly before serving, cook spaghetti in salted, boiling water. Place a serving of spaghetti on each plate and cover with sauce.

Yield: 8 servings

Recipe:...
INGREDIENTS:.....................................
....
....
....

DIRECTIONS:.......................................
....
....
....
....

YIELD:..

Recipe:...
INGREDIENTS:.....................................
....
....
....

DIRECTIONS:.......................................
....
....
....
....

YIELD:..

Recipe:...
INGREDIENTS:...
....
....
DIRECTIONS:...
....
....
....
....
YIELD:...

Recipe:...
INGREDIENTS:...
....
....
DIRECTIONS:...
....
....
....
....
YIELD:...

Recipe:...
INGREDIENTS:...
....
....
DIRECTIONS:...
....
....
....
....
YIELD:...

On the tenth day of Christmas my true love sent to me. . .

Ten Salads a-Crunching

Christmas is a day of meaning and
traditions, a special day spent in the
warm circle of family and friends.

Margaret Thatcher

Dear Lord Jesus, thank You for sharing
Your birthday with us. As we celebrate
Your advent, we ask that You transform
our hearts, making them suitable
gifts to lay before You. Amen.

❋ · ❋ · ✳ · ❋ · ❋ · ✳

*For unto you is born this day in the city
of David a Saviour, which is Christ the Lord.*

LUKE 2:11

Cranberry Rice Salad

1½ cups cooked white rice

½ cup cooked wild rice

½ cup dried cranberries

¼ cup chopped parsley

½ teaspoon salt

½ teaspoon pepper

2 tablespoons olive oil

1 tablespoon chopped green onions

¼ teaspoon ground cloves

In large bowl, combine white and wild rice, cranberries, parsley, salt, pepper, olive oil, onions, and cloves. Refrigerate. Can be served warm or cold.

YIELD: 6 SERVINGS

Mushroom, Artichoke, and Spinach Salad

8 ounces bacon, crisply cooked and crumbled

3 hard-boiled eggs, sliced

1 (9 ounce) package artichoke hearts

8 ounces mushrooms, sliced

1 pound fresh spinach, stemmed and washed

1½ cups blue cheese dressing

In serving bowl, combine bacon, eggs, artichoke hearts, mushrooms, and spinach. Chill. Just before serving, place salad on serving plates and top with dressing.

YIELD: 6 SERVINGS

Day-after Turkey Salad

❄ · ❄ · ❄ · ❄ · ❄ · ❄

3 cups diced turkey

1 cup chopped celery

1 cup bean sprouts

1 cup toasted almonds, sliced

2 cups leftover turkey stuffing

½ cup mayonnaise

½ cup sour cream

6 lettuce wedges

In large bowl, mix turkey, celery, sprouts, almonds, stuffing, mayonnaise, and sour cream. Blend well. Chill. Just before serving, place lettuce wedges on serving plates. Add salad.

YIELD: 6 SERVINGS

Golden Pineapple Salad

❄ · ❄ · ❄ · ❄ · ❄ · ❄

2 tablespoons unflavored gelatin

⅓ cup cold water

1 cup unsweetened pineapple juice

⅓ cup honey

¾ cup orange juice

¼ cup lemon juice

1 cup coarsely grated carrot

1 cup orange sections, cut up

1½ cups unsweetened crushed pineapple, drained

Soften gelatin in water. Heat pineapple juice in microwave. Add gelatin. Stir until dissolved. Stir in honey. Blend well. Add orange juice and lemon juice. Cool in refrigerator until mixture begins to thicken. Fold in carrots, orange sections, and pineapple. Return to refrigerator until ready to serve.

YIELD: 6 SERVINGS

Mandarin Orange Salad

❄ · ❄ · ❄ · ❄ · ❄

2 (3 ounce) boxes orange gelatin

1 cup boiling water

2 cups orange sherbet

1 large can mandarin oranges, drained

1 cup heavy cream, whipped

Dissolve gelatin in boiling water. Stir in sherbet until melted. Chill until thick and cool but not set, then fold in oranges and whipped cream. Pour into mold or serving bowl. Refrigerate for 2 hours or until well set.

Yield: 8 servings

Fruit-Cheese Salad

2 large heads lettuce, torn into pieces

4 ounces sliced sharp cheddar cheese, cut into thin strips

½ cup sliced celery

⅔ cup oil

⅓ cup wine vinegar

½ cup sugar

2 teaspoons grated onion

1 teaspoon dry mustard

½ teaspoon salt

1 (11 ounce) can mandarin orange sections

1 (8 ounce) can jellied cranberry sauce, chilled, cut into cubes

1 avocado, peeled and sliced

In salad bowl, combine lettuce, cheese, and celery; set aside. In small bowl, combine oil, vinegar, sugar, onion, mustard, and salt. Pour over lettuce mixture to coat. Add orange sections, cranberry sauce, and avocado slices. Toss gently.

YIELD: 12 SERVINGS

Cheery Cherry Fruit Salad

1 (8 ounce) can cherry pie filling

1 (14 ounce) can sweetened condensed milk

1 (8 ounce) can pineapple chunks

½ cup nuts

1 (8 ounce) container whipped topping

In serving bowl, mix together pie filling, condensed milk, pineapple chunks, and nuts. Fold in whipped topping. Chill and serve. Best if refrigerated overnight.

YIELD: 10 SERVINGS

Merry Macaroni Salad

16 ounces shell macaroni

1 green bell pepper, chopped

4 carrots, chopped

1 purple onion, chopped

1 cup celery, chopped

½ cup sunflower seeds

8 to 10 slices bacon, cooked and crumbled

1 pound processed cheese, cubed

½ cup sour cream

1½ cups mayonnaise

1 teaspoon lemon juice

Cook macaroni in salted, boiling water until tender. Drain and cool. In serving bowl, combine macaroni, pepper, carrots, onion, celery, sunflower seeds, bacon, cheese, sour cream, mayonnaise, and lemon juice. Mix well and chill.

Yield: 8 servings

Marinated Bean Salad

2 cups cooked cut green beans

1 cup cooked or canned chickpeas

1 cup cooked or canned kidney
beans

1 cup cooked or canned lima beans

1 red onion, sliced

1 carrot, shredded

1 cup Italian dressing

½ teaspoon salt

¼ teaspoon pepper

In serving bowl, combine green beans, chickpeas, kidney beans, lima beans, onion, and carrot. Pour dressing over salad and season with salt and pepper. Chill. Serve on bed of lettuce or greens.

YIELD: 6 TO 8 SERVINGS

Festive Chicken Salad

1 cup green grapes

1 cup chopped celery

1 cup crushed pineapple

1 cup slivered almonds

4 cups chicken, cubed

½ cup sour cream

1½ cups mayonnaise

1 tablespoon lemon juice

In serving bowl, combine grapes, celery, pineapple, almonds, chicken, sour cream, mayonnaise, and lemon juice. Gently blend together. Refrigerate until ready to serve.

YIELD: 6 TO 8 SERVINGS

North Pole Banana Salad

4 ripe bananas, mashed

1 cup sugar

1½ cups buttermilk

1 (8 ounce) carton whipped topping

1 head lettuce

Mix together bananas, sugar, buttermilk, and whipped topping. Pour into 9x12-inch baking dish. Freeze. Just before serving, remove from freezer, cut into small squares, and place on lettuce leaf to serve.

YIELD: 10 SERVINGS

Cucumber and Onion Salad

❋ · ❋ · ❋ · ❋ · ❋ · ❋

1 large cucumber

1 large onion

1 teaspoon salt

1 teaspoon sugar

⅓ cup cider vinegar

½ cup water

Ice cubes

Peel cucumber and score sides. Slice cucumber and onion into a bowl. Sprinkle with salt and sugar. Cover with cider vinegar and water. Cover with ice cubes. Chill for 30 minutes. Transfer to serving bowl.

Yield: 6 servings

White Christmas Salad

❋ · ❋ · ❋ · ❋ · ❋ · ❋

1 small head cauliflower

1 medium onion, sliced

1 white radish, sliced

1 small cucumber, sliced

1 cup sour cream

2 teaspoons lemon juice

2 tablespoons sugar

½ teaspoon salt

¼ teaspoon coarsely ground pepper

1 small head lettuce

In serving bowl, break cauliflower into flowerets. Add onion, radish, and cucumber. Toss; set aside. In small bowl, combine sour cream, lemon juice, sugar, salt, and pepper. Pour over salad. Allow to marinate for 1 hour. Serve over lettuce leaves.

Yield: 6 servings

Walnut Salad

4 heads Boston lettuce

⅔ cups walnut oil

⅓ cup fresh lemon juice

½ teaspoon Dijon mustard

¾ teaspoon sugar

½ teaspoon salt

¼ teaspoon pepper

1 large egg white

1 tablespoon water

1 cup brown sugar, firmly packed

1½ cups walnuts

2 ounces blue cheese, crumbled

1 apple, peeled, cored, cut into thin slices

Preheat oven to 300 degrees. In large bowl, tear lettuce into pieces and set aside. Combine walnut oil, lemon juice, mustard, sugar, salt, and pepper in covered jar. Shake well and refrigerate. In medium bowl, beat egg white and water until frothy. Add brown sugar and stir until sugar dissolves. Add walnuts and toss to coat. Spread walnuts in single layer on ungreased baking sheet. Bake for 8 minutes, stirring occasionally. Cool. Add to lettuce, along with blue cheese and apple slices. Add dressing and toss before serving.

YIELD: 6 TO 8 SERVINGS

Christmas Cornbread Salad

1¼ cups flour

¾ cup cornmeal

¼ cup sugar

2 teaspoons baking powder

¼ cup oil

1 egg, beaten

1 onion, chopped

1 green bell pepper, chopped

1 carrot, grated

1 cup chopped celery

1 cup tomatoes, chopped

1 cup mayonnaise

Preheat oven to 400 degrees. In medium bowl, combine flour, cornmeal, sugar, baking powder, oil, and egg. Pour into greased 8-inch baking pan. Bake for 25 minutes. Cool. In large salad bowl, crumble cornbread. Add onion, pepper, carrot, celery, and tomatoes. Toss together. Add mayonnaise. Mix well.

YIELD: 6 TO 8 SERVINGS

Cool Ranch Coleslaw

2 (16 ounce) packages shredded cabbage slaw

1 tablespoon cider vinegar

1 (16 ounce) bottle ranch-style dressing

1 tablespoon mayonnaise

1 cup sugar

½ teaspoon salt

¼ teaspoon pepper

In large serving bowl, combine 1 bag of slaw with vinegar, dressing, mayonnaise, sugar, salt, and pepper. Fold ingredients together until well blended. Add remaining bag of slaw. Stir until well blended.

YIELD: 10 TO 12 SERVINGS

Recipe: ....

INGREDIENTS: ....

....

....

DIRECTIONS: ....

....

....

....

....

YIELD: ....

Recipe: ....

INGREDIENTS: ....

....

....

DIRECTIONS: ....

....

....

....

....

YIELD: ....

Recipe:

INGREDIENTS:

DIRECTIONS:

YIELD:

Recipe:

INGREDIENTS:

DIRECTIONS:

YIELD:

Recipe:

INGREDIENTS:

DIRECTIONS:

YIELD:

On the eleventh day of Christmas my true love sent to me. . .

Eleven Sides a-Steaming

Nations have their red letter days, their
carnivals and festivals, but once in a year
and only once, the whole world stands
still to celebrate the advent of a life.

AUTHOR UNKNOWN

Jesus, You are the most important person who ever lived. Your life, death, and resurrection open—for me and for the whole world—the pathway to eternal life. Amen.

Rejoice greatly, O daughter of Zion; shout, O daughter of Jerusalem: behold, thy King cometh unto thee: he is just, and having salvation.

ZECHARIAH 9:9

Hearty Baked Beans

2 cans Great Northern beans,
   drained and rinsed

2 tablespoons dried minced onions

½ teaspoon salt

½ teaspoon pepper

½ cup ketchup

2 tablespoons molasses

½ cup brown sugar

1 teaspoon mustard

2 teaspoons cider vinegar

4 strips bacon, cooked and
   crumbled

Preheat oven to 350 degrees. In large bowl, stir together beans, onion, salt, pepper, ketchup, molasses, sugar, mustard, and vinegar. Pour into baking dish. Sprinkle with bacon. Bake for 30 minutes or until bubbly.

YIELD: 6 SERVINGS

Creamed Onions

3 cups canned baby onions, drained

4 tablespoons butter

4 tablespoons flour

1 cup whole milk

1 cup half-and-half

1 teaspoon salt

½ teaspoon pepper

Preheat oven to 350 degrees. Place onions in greased 1-quart baking dish; set aside. In heavy saucepan, whisk together butter, flour, milk, half-and-half, salt, and pepper. Stir until thickened. Pour over onions and bake for 15 minutes.

YIELD: 6 SERVINGS

Colorful Carrots

6 large carrots, scraped and cut into
  thick rounds

¼ cup butter

¼ cup sugar

3 navel oranges, sectioned

2 tablespoons grated orange zest

In saucepan, cook carrots in boiling water for 20 minutes or until tender.
Drain. Add butter and sugar and stir over medium heat until carrots are
lightly glazed. Just before serving, stir in orange sections and zest.

YIELD: 6 SERVINGS

Cheesy Brussels Sprouts

1½ pounds brussels sprouts,
  trimmed and cut in half

⅓ cup butter

1 cup cheddar cheese crackers,
  crushed

¼ cup grated Parmesan cheese

In saucepan, cover sprouts with water. Cover and simmer for 15 minutes
or until crisp and tender. Drain. Keep warm. In skillet, melt butter over low
heat. Add crackers and stir until golden brown. Remove from heat and stir in
cheese. Pour sprouts into serving dish and sprinkle with cracker crumbs.

YIELD: 6 SERVINGS

Gingered Beets

1 (16 ounce) can sliced beets,
   drained

½ cup sugar

1 tablespoon cornstarch

¾ teaspoon ginger

¼ teaspoon salt

½ cup cider vinegar

2 tablespoons butter

1 tablespoon chopped parsley

In saucepan, combine beets, sugar, cornstarch, ginger, and salt. Blend well. Add vinegar. Stirring constantly, bring to a rapid boil. Cook for 3 minutes. Add butter. Cover and simmer over low heat for 10 minutes, turning occasionally. Transfer to serving dish. Sprinkle with parsley.

YIELD: 4 SERVINGS

Mushroom Delight

1 pound mushrooms, cleaned and sliced

¼ cup butter

½ clove garlic, minced

2 tablespoons minced parsley

½ teaspoon salt

⅛ teaspoon pepper

1 cup sour cream

1 tablespoon flour

6 slices toasted bread, cubed

Place mushrooms and butter in skillet over low heat for 1 minute. Add garlic, parsley, salt, and pepper. Raise temperature to medium; cook until tender and lightly browned, turning occasionally. Add sour cream and flour. Cook for 5 minutes, stirring constantly until sauce is slightly thick and thoroughly heated. Do not boil. Serve with toast.

YIELD: 6 SERVINGS

Parmesan Potato Croquettes

2 cups mashed potatoes

2 tablespoons minced onion

1 egg, slightly beaten

3 tablespoons grated Parmesan
   cheese

2 tablespoons parsley, minced

¾ cup bread crumbs

2 tablespoons vegetable oil

In medium bowl, combine potatoes, onion, egg, cheese, and parsley. Blend thoroughly. Shape into 8 patties. Place in refrigerator for 1 hour. Pour bread crumbs onto waxed paper. Dip patties in crumbs, coating each side; set aside. In large skillet, heat oil on moderate heat. Place croquettes in skillet and cook for 4 minutes or until evenly browned on each side.

YIELD: 4 TO 6 SERVINGS

Christmas Corn Casserole

1 (12 ounce) box cornbread mix

1 (12 ounce) can cream-style corn

1 (12 ounce) can whole kernel corn,
   drained

2 eggs, beaten

½ cup butter, melted

1 cup sour cream

½ cup grated cheddar cheese

Preheat oven to 350 degrees. Combine cornbread mix, corn, eggs, butter, sour cream, and cheese. Mix well. Pour into greased 2-quart casserole dish. Bake for 25 minutes or until golden brown.

YIELD: 6 SERVINGS

Papa's Squash Casserole

3 pounds zucchini or yellow squash

½ cup butter

1 (.4 ounce) package ranch-style dressing mix

2 eggs, slightly beaten

¼ teaspoon salt

⅛ teaspoon pepper

2 cups grated cheddar cheese, divided

1 (8 ounce) package cream cheese, softened

Preheat oven to 350 degrees. Cut squash into chunks. In skillet, sauté squash in butter until barely tender. Drain and mash; place in large bowl. Add dressing mix, eggs, salt, pepper, 1 cup cheddar cheese, and cream cheese. Blend well. Pour into 2-quart greased casserole pan. Sprinkle remaining cheese on top. Bake for 20 minutes or until golden brown.

YIELD: 6 TO 8 SERVINGS

Broccoli, Rice, and Cheese Casserole

❄ · ❄ · ❄ · ❄ · ❄

3 cups cooked brown or white rice

1 (10 ounce) package frozen broccoli, thawed

1 (10.75 ounce) can cream of mushroom soup

4 ounces cream cheese, softened

¾ cup grated sharp cheddar cheese

½ cup butter, melted

Preheat oven to 350 degrees. In large bowl, combine rice, broccoli, soup, cream cheese, cheddar cheese, and butter. Mix well. Pour into long, buttered casserole dish. Bake for 35 minutes or until cheese is bubbling.

YIELD: 6 TO 8 SERVINGS

Three Vegetable Combo

1 (12 ounce) package frozen
  brussels sprouts

1 (12 ounce) package frozen
  chopped broccoli

1 (12 ounce) package frozen
  cauliflower

1 (8 ounce) jar processed cheese

8 ounces cream of mushroom soup

Preheat oven to 350 degrees. In large bowl, combine sprouts, broccoli, cauliflower, cheese, and soup. Mix well. Place in 2-quart greased casserole dish. Bake for 45 minutes, stirring occasionally.

Yield: 12 servings

Peas and Onions

1 (16 ounce) jar baby onions,
  drained

1 (16 ounce) can green peas,
  undrained

⅓ cup butter

¼ teaspoon salt

⅛ teaspoon pepper

2 tablespoons chopped fresh parsley

In medium saucepan, combine onions and peas. Heat thoroughly over medium heat. Drain. Add butter and stir until melted. Season with salt and pepper. Pour into serving dish and sprinkle with parsley.

Yield: 6 servings

Spinach Casserole

* · * · · * · * · · *

1 (10 ounce) package frozen
   chopped spinach

⅓ cup chopped onion

¼ cup butter

1 (10.75 ounce) can cream of
   mushroom soup

1 (8 ounce) package cream cheese

3 eggs, separated (reserve whites)

1 teaspoon garlic powder

¼ cup Parmesan cheese

¼ teaspoon salt

⅛ teaspoon pepper

½ cup bread crumbs

Preheat oven to 350 degrees. Cook spinach in salted, boiling water for 3
minutes. Drain well and set aside. In large saucepan, sauté onion in butter.
Add soup and cream cheese to onion mixture. Stir until melted. Cool. Add
egg yolks, garlic powder, Parmesan cheese, salt, and pepper. Blend well. Add
spinach to soup mixture; set aside. In bowl, beat egg whites until stiff. Fold
into spinach mixture. Pour into greased 1-quart casserole dish. Top with
bread crumbs.

Yield: 8 servings

Garlic Rosemary Roasted Potatoes

* · * · * · * · *

1½ pounds small new potatoes, scrubbed and dried

¼ cup extra-virgin olive oil

1½ teaspoons garlic powder

1 tablespoon fresh or dried rosemary

1 teaspoon salt

¼ teaspoon pepper

Preheat oven to 350 degrees. Cut potatoes in half. In large bowl, mix oil and seasonings. Add potatoes. Blend well. Transfer potatoes to shallow baking dish. Bake for 40 minutes or until tender.

YIELD: 8 SERVINGS

Bessie's Best Baked Rice

½ cup butter

1½ cups uncooked rice

4 green onions with tops, sliced

2 (10½ ounce) cans condensed beef bouillon

1 (4 ounce) can sliced mushrooms, drained

Preheat oven to 375 degrees. In large skillet, melt butter. Add rice and onions. Sauté until rice is golden brown. Add bouillon and mushrooms, stirring well. Pour into greased 1-quart casserole dish. Cover and bake for 1 hour.

YIELD: 8 SERVINGS

Dilled Zucchini and Carrots

1 medium onion, chopped

1 tablespoon butter

3 medium zucchini

1 large carrot, sliced

½ teaspoon dill weed

¼ teaspoon salt

1 tablespoon water

In large skillet, sauté onion in butter for 2 minutes. Add zucchini, carrot, dill weed, salt, and water. Cook for 5 minutes over medium heat. Stir occasionally. Reduce heat to low and simmer for 10 minutes or until vegetables are tender.

YIELD: 6 SERVINGS

Cheesy Baked Cauliflower

1 medium head cauliflower, broken into bite-size flowerets

¼ teaspoon salt

1 cup water

1 (10.75 ounce) can condensed cheddar cheese soup

⅓ cup milk

⅛ teaspoon paprika

3 tablespoons butter, melted

¼ cup dry bread crumbs

Preheat oven to 350 degrees. Place cauliflower in salted, boiling water for 3 minutes. Reduce to simmer and cook until tender. Drain well. Blend soup, milk, and paprika in separate bowl. Place cauliflower in buttered, 2-quart casserole dish and pour sauce over top. Mix butter with bread crumbs and sprinkle over top of sauce. Bake for 15 minutes.

Yield: 8 servings

Fabulous Cabbage

1 medium head cabbage, chopped

1 onion, chopped

1 tablespoon butter

1 (10.75 ounce) can cream of
mushroom soup

½ cup cubed processed cheese

½ teaspoon salt

¼ teaspoon pepper

1 cup bread crumbs

2 tablespoons butter, melted

Preheat oven to 350 degrees. In skillet, sauté cabbage and onion in butter for 10 minutes. Do not overcook cabbage. In large saucepan, combine soup and cheese. Stir until cheese is melted. Add cabbage mixture. Add salt and pepper. Stir. Pour into greased 2-quart casserole dish. Top with bread crumbs and drizzle with butter. Bake for 30 minutes.

Yield: 8 servings

Candied Sweet Potatoes

6 medium sweet potatoes, peeled

½ cup butter, melted

½ cup brown sugar

½ cup white sugar

¼ cup water

1 teaspoon salt

Peel and slice sweet potatoes ½-inch thick. In skillet or saucepan, combine butter, sugars, water, and salt. Combine well. Add sweet potatoes. Stir until well coated. Cover and simmer for 1 hour or until done, turning frequently.

YIELD: 6 TO 8 SERVINGS

Bleu Cheese Asparagus

1 pound asparagus spears

1 (3 ounce) package cream cheese, softened

6 tablespoons evaporated milk

¼ teaspoon salt

⅛ teaspoon white pepper

3 tablespoons blue cheese, crumbled

Cook asparagus in salted, boiling water until tender. Drain and set aside. In small saucepan, combine cream cheese, milk, salt, and pepper. Cook over low heat until smooth. Stir in cheese and heat thoroughly. Place asparagus on plate and top with sauce.

YIELD: 4 TO 6 SERVINGS

My Favorite Christmas Side Dish Recipes

Recipe:

INGREDIENTS:

DIRECTIONS:

YIELD:

Recipe:

INGREDIENTS:

DIRECTIONS:

YIELD:

Recipe:..

INGREDIENTS:..

....

....

DIRECTIONS:..

....

....

....

....

YIELD:..

Recipe:..

INGREDIENTS:..

....

....

DIRECTIONS:..

....

....

....

....

YIELD:..

Recipe:..

INGREDIENTS:..

....

....

DIRECTIONS:..

....

....

....

....

YIELD:..

On the twelfth day of Christmas my true love sent to me. . .

Twelve Soups a-Simmering

As long as we know in our hearts
what Christmas ought to be, Christmas is.

ERIC SEVAREID

Dear Father, bless our hands this Christmas season as we wrap presents, prepare Christmas goodies, decorate the tree, and fold them in appreciation for all Your great gifts. Amen.

Now the God of hope fill you with all joy and peace in believing, that ye may abound in hope, through the power of the Holy Ghost.

ROMANS 15:13

Chicken Enchilada Soup

1 (16 ounce) package
processed cheese

1 (10¾ ounce) can cream of
chicken soup

1 (15 ounce) can black beans,
drained

1 (7 ounce) can extra-sweet corn

1 (14 ounce) can diced tomatoes
with chilies

1 (16 ounce) jar salsa (not chunky)

1 cup milk

½ cup crushed tortilla chips

1 avocado, sliced, for garnish

6 teaspoons sour cream, for garnish

Cube cheese. In soup pot, combine cheese with chicken soup, beans, corn, tomatoes, salsa, milk, and chips. Cook over moderate heat until cheese melts. Reduce heat. Simmer on low and stir frequently until soup is smooth. Keep warm. Just before serving, garnish with avocado slice and teaspoon of sour cream.

YIELD: 6 TO 8 SERVINGS

Home for the Holidays Pumpkin Soup

½ cup minced onions

2 tablespoons oil

3 cups chicken broth, divided

3 cups pumpkin puree

¼ teaspoon nutmeg

1 cup croutons for garnish

In small skillet, sauté onions in oil until golden but not brown. In blender, combine onions with 1 cup chicken broth. Blend until pureed. In heavy saucepan, combine onion mixture, remaining broth, and pumpkin puree. Heat. Add nutmeg. Serve with croutons.

YIELD: 4 SERVINGS

Butternut Squash Bisque

1 large butternut squash, halved and
seeded

½ cup butter

¼ teaspoon salt

⅛ teaspoon pepper

1 small onion, diced

4 cups chicken stock

1 teaspoon celery salt

1 teaspoon paprika

1 cup heavy cream

1 cup sour cream

3 slices bacon, cooked and
crumbled

Preheat oven to 350 degrees. Bake squash for 35 minutes. Cool. Scoop meat
into large soup pot. Add butter, salt, pepper, onion, chicken stock, celery
salt, and paprika. Simmer for 20 minutes. Cool. Pour into blender and
process until smooth. Return to soup pot. Add heavy cream. Reheat, but do
not boil. Garnish with sour cream and bacon.

YIELD: 8 SERVINGS

Cream of Mushroom Soup

3 cups shiitake mushrooms, finely diced

½ cup chopped leeks

1 teaspoon minced garlic

1 tablespoon butter

2 tablespoons flour

4 cups milk, divided

2 tablespoons cooking sherry

1 tablespoon chopped fresh parsley

2 tablespoons chicken stock concentrate

¼ teaspoon thyme

1 teaspoon salt

1 teaspoon pepper

In large soup pot, sauté mushrooms, leeks, and garlic in butter until tender. In small bowl, dissolve flour in 1 cup milk. Add to sautéed vegetables, along with remaining milk, sherry, parsley, chicken stock, thyme, salt, and pepper. Stir constantly over medium heat as soup thickens. Simmer on low heat for 30 minutes.

YIELD: 8 SERVINGS

Festive Tomato Soup

1 teaspoon vegetable oil

1 medium onion, diced

1 (27 ounce) can diced tomatoes

¾ cup water

½ tablespoon brown sugar

1 teaspoon salt

1 teaspoon pepper

½ cup sour cream

¼ cup chives

Heat oil in soup pot over medium heat. Add onion and sauté for 3 minutes. Add tomatoes, water, brown sugar, salt, and pepper. Bring to boil. Reduce heat and simmer on low for 5 minutes. Garnish with sour cream and chives.

YIELD: 4 SERVINGS

South of the Border Holiday Soup

1 (16 ounce) can black beans

1 (16 ounce) can pinto beans

1 (14.5 ounce) can diced tomatoes

1 (15 ounce) can sweet corn

1 (12.5 ounce) can chicken breast

1 (10¾ ounce) can cream of chicken soup

1 (10 ounce) can enchilada sauce

1 (14 ounce) can chicken broth

1 package taco seasoning

1 avocado, sliced, for garnish

Drain beans, tomatoes, and corn. Pour into slow-cooker. Add chicken, soup, enchilada sauce, chicken broth, and seasoning. Blend well. Cook on low for 3 hours. Garnish with avocado slice.

YIELD: 8 TO 10 SERVINGS

Creamy Broccoli Cheddar Soup

✳ · ✳ · ✳ · ✳ · ✳

6 tablespoons butter

1 small onion, chopped

⅓ cup flour

1 cup heavy whipping cream

1 (13¾ ounce) can chicken broth

¼ teaspoon ground nutmeg

⅛ teaspoon ground thyme

1 teaspoon salt

⅛ teaspoon ground white pepper

¼ teaspoon garlic powder

3 cups bite-size broccoli florets

1 cup milk

¼ teaspoon Worcestershire sauce

1 cup shredded sharp white or
   yellow cheddar cheese

½ cup shredded Havarti cheese

½ cup shredded swiss cheese

In large saucepan, melt butter over low heat. Add onion. Cook until tender.
Whisk in flour and cook for 3 minutes or until golden. Gradually whisk
in cream until smooth. Add broth and spices. Bring to simmer and cook,
stirring constantly, until thickened. Stir in broccoli. Simmer for 10 minutes.
Remove from heat. Stir in milk and Worcestershire sauce. Add cheeses. Stir
until melted.

YIELD: 6 TO 8 SERVINGS

Oyster Bisque

1 cup finely chopped celery

2 cups water

1 pint oysters, finely chopped
(retain liquid)

1 tablespoon butter

1 tablespoon flour

1 quart milk

½ teaspoon salt

¼ teaspoon pepper

Boil celery in water for 30 minutes. Drain and set aside. Cook oysters in their own juice for 10 minutes; set aside. Melt butter in top of double boiler. Add flour and stir. Add milk gradually. Stir on medium heat until smooth. Add celery and oysters. Season with salt and pepper. Cook for 20 minutes.

Yield: 6 servings

Pumpkin Corn Soup

* · * · * · * · * ·

32 ounces chicken broth

2 (15 ounce) cans pumpkin puree

2 teaspoons garlic, minced

2 teaspoons nutmeg

2 teaspoons thyme

2 tablespoons brown sugar

½ onion, chopped

1 tablespoon olive oil

1½ cups heavy cream

1 (14.5 ounce) can corn, drained

1 teaspoon salt

¼ teaspoon pepper

½ cup pumpkin seeds, for garnish

In large saucepan, place chicken broth. Add pumpkin, garlic, spices, and brown sugar. Cook on low heat until mixture is warm and well blended. In skillet, sauté onion in olive oil until caramelized. Add to soup mixture. Add cream and corn. Using hand blender, mix until smooth. Add salt and pepper. Mix well. Pour into bowls and top with pumpkin seeds.

YIELD: 5 SERVINGS

· ·

Peanut Butter Soup

* · * · * · * · * ·

1 tablespoon butter

1 small onion, chopped

1 teaspoon flour

1 cup peanut butter

4 cups milk

1 teaspoon salt

½ teaspoon pepper

In skillet, melt butter and sauté onion until delicate brown. Using whisk, incorporate flour. Add peanut butter and cook for 3 to 4 minutes. Scald milk in double boiler; season with salt and pepper. Strain peanut butter mixture into milk. Cook for 10 to 15 minutes.

YIELD: 6 SERVINGS

White Christmas Chili

3 (15 ounce) cans Great Northern or white kidney beans, rinsed and drained

2½ cups chopped cooked chicken

1½ cups chopped red or green bell pepper

1 cup chopped onion

2 fresh jalapeno chili peppers, seeded and chopped

2 teaspoons ground cumin

2 cloves garlic, minced

½ teaspoon salt

½ teaspoon dried oregano

3½ cups chicken broth

1 cup shredded Monterey Jack cheese for garnish

In large slow-cooker, combine beans, chicken, bell pepper, onion, jalapeno peppers, cumin, garlic, salt, and oregano. Blend well. Pour broth over mixture. Cover and cook on low for 8 to 10 hours or on high for 4 to 5 hours. Garnish with cheese.

YIELD: 8 SERVINGS

Recipe: ....

INGREDIENTS: ....

....

....

DIRECTIONS: ....

....

....

....

....

YIELD: ....

Recipe: ....

INGREDIENTS: ....

....

....

DIRECTIONS: ....

....

....

....

YIELD: ....

Recipe:..

INGREDIENTS:...

....

....

DIRECTIONS:..

....

....

....

....

YIELD:...

Recipe:..

INGREDIENTS:...

....

....

DIRECTIONS:..

....

....

....

....

YIELD:...

Recipe:..

INGREDIENTS:...

....

....

DIRECTIONS:..

....

....

....

....

YIELD:...

Index

APPETIZERS

BEVERAGES

BREADS

BREAKFAST DISHES

CANDIES

COOKIES

DESSERTS

KIDS' RECIPES

MAIN DISHES

SALADS

SIDES

SOUPS

Recipe Notes